Le Marais

A Rare Steakhouse...Well Done

Mark Hennessey

Jose Meirelles

gefen גפן
publishing house בית הוצאה לאור
JERUSALEM ● NEW YORK Est. 1981

Copyright © 2016 Mitico, Inc
Jerusalem 2016/5776

Cover design: Diane Liff, D. Liff Graphics
Typesetting: Renana Typesetting
Photographs taken by Martim Meirelles

ISBN: 978-965-229-636-8

1 3 5 7 9 8 6 4 2

Gefen Publishing House Ltd.

6 Hatzvi Street
Jerusalem 94386, Israel
972-2-538-0247
orders@gefenpublishing.com

Gefen Books

11 Edison Place
Springfield, NJ 07081
516-593-1234
orders@gefenpublishing.com

www.gefenpublishing.com

Printed in Israel

Send for our free catalog

Library of Congress Cataloging-in-Publication Data

Hennessey, Mark, author.
  Le Marais : a rare steakhouse...well done / Mark Hennessey, Jose Meirelles.
    pages cm
  ISBN 978-965-229-636-8
  1. Cooking, French. 2. Jewish cooking. 3. Le Marais (Restaurant) I. Meirelles, Jose, author. II. Title.
  TX724.2.F74H46 2016
  641.5944–dc23
                                    2015015078

Contents

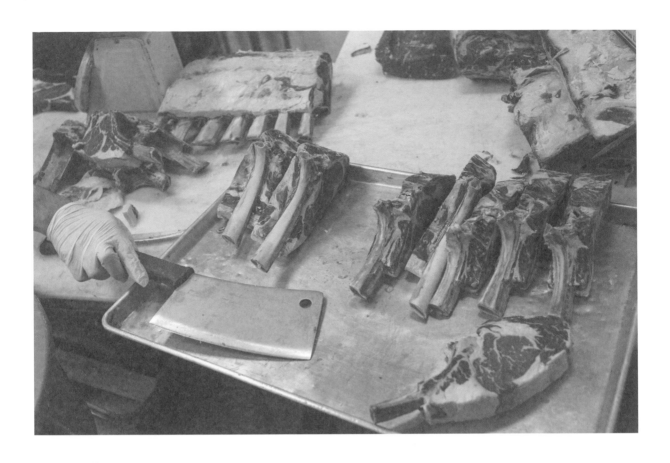

Foreword

When Jose Meirelles asked us to write an introduction to his new cookbook, our first thought was that it was a strange but interesting request. We were fascinated, to be sure, and we enjoy good food, but we are certainly not food critics. Then another thought occurred to us. Jose's story is very much a part of why we love New York City.

New York is a vibrant place in which almost anything is possible; a place in which "If I can make it there, I can make it anywhere" is not just a lyric, but a way of life.

Jose Meirelles' Brasserie Le Marais is one of the proofs of that. This restaurant epitomizes the New York story. Where else would a non-Jewish Portuguese immigrant open a French bistro, hire an Irish-Italian Catholic as its executive chef, and create one of the finest and most successful kosher restaurants in the United States? Jose's story is a classic New York story; it personifies the New York ethos. And it's proof of the growth of the observant Jewish community in America that wants to "eat out" at high-quality kosher restaurants.

So we decided to write this introduction to the Le Marais cookbook.

Once upon a time our friend and former Senate colleague Chris Dodd told us that he had just been to New York to meet with some people for dinner. They took him to an elegantly styled little eatery in the theater district. Chris got quickly to his table, sat facing his guests, and was oblivious to the other diners in the room.

The meal, he said, was fantastic. His seared steak was perfect and the entire meal was delicious, but he thought little of that because that kind of meal is to be expected in New York restaurants.

When he and his guests stood up to leave, however, Chris noticed for the first time that many of the diners were wearing skull caps. A light bulb went off. "It was a kosher restaurant," he told me, somewhat in amazement. Chris said he had not often had a steak as good as the one he had that night.

That delighted us because he was extolling the virtues of a kosher restaurant, Le Marais. He was putting its cuisine on a par with other restaurants he considered to be among the best.

By then, we were not strangers to Brasserie Le Marais. In fact, we were already fans. Over the years we have seen the phenomenal growth of kosher eateries especially in New York. It was not always thus. It used to be much harder to find quality kosher restaurants to take prospective friends or, in my case, supporters.

Le Marais was one of the first of the new generation of excellent kosher restaurants. So when we were in New York, we would hold as many events as we could upstairs in Le Marais, or we would make use of its catering services. It has a terrific ambiance, with an old-fashioned French steakhouse feel that is elegant and comfortable.

Although Le Marais was one of the first to break through, we now live in an unprecedented golden age of kosher restaurants which Le Marais helped bring about.

Le Marais was probably the first kosher steak house to offer dry-aged meats. We are not authorities on the meat-aging process, but if taste is an indicator, we would have to say the cuts at Le Marais are tender and quite good – and noticeably different from non-aged meats we find elsewhere.

Then there are the wines. Not only is Jose a great chef, but he has a nose and palate for fine wine, as well, and he makes a point of helping choose wines that match the food. It is relatively new for kosher diners to be able to enjoy fine kosher wines with kosher aged steaks. Jose has brought both to 46th Street.

Restaurant reviewers, whose reputations are built on knowing the good from the bad, and the great from the good, agree with our opinion of Le Marais. Thus, writing in *New York Magazine*, Michael Anstendig called Le Marais' meat "the main attraction." A "working butcher shop at the entrance and on-premise aging room signal that these folks mean business," he wrote. "Cuts of succulent rib eye and prime rib are all ably prepared; shallot and bearnaise sauces add further perk. Fabulous fries complete the picture. Other specialties range from steak tartare to slow-cooked veal and from beef burgundy to chicken fricassee. There's more to kosher than pastrami, after all." That is why we said yes when Jose asked us to write the introduction to his new cookbook.

Le Marais is a unique restaurant. It has remained popular for so long because the food, wine, and service are so good. It just also happens to be kosher.

Hadassah and Joe Lieberman

The Le Marais Story

As an avid reader and owner of cookbooks, I am always interested in reading the story behind the restaurant. Just like every person has their own interesting life story, so does each business. What is in the DNA of the business that makes it thrive where so many others have failed? As a chef, I find these stories informative as well as inspirational. Wait! Don't look away! This is generally the boring filler at the beginning of a book put there by the publisher to indulge the authors and give them that sense of importance needed to complete a project of this size. I get it, where's the damn prime-rib recipe that I paid for? Stay with me just a bit more, because the story of Le Marais is a classic New York story. Where else but in New York City does a Portuguese immigrant have the guts to open a kosher steakhouse on the biggest possible stage and then have the absolute gall to make it the most successful restaurant of its kind in the country? How dare he! Oh, but he did, and nearly 20 years later that very same restaurant is not only stronger than ever, but more dedicated than ever to providing the best kosher fare that there is to offer.

In 1995, Jose Meirelles and Philippe Lajaunie were partners of a very popular French brasserie on Park Avenue called Les Halles. At that time, Philippe had opened a restaurant in the Paramount Hotel and was having some legal wrangles with the legendary hotelier Ian Shrager. During his frequent meetings with his lawyers, they were needling Philippe to open a restaurant similar to Les Halles, but kosher. Jose's initial reaction was, "Are you kidding?!" (For what it's worth, my initial reaction also.) "How could I operate a French restaurant without cheese, shellfish, and butter for finishing sauces? Pork!!!!" Not to mention that from a business perspective, closing on Friday and Saturday was pure death. And let's face it, kosher meat didn't exactly have the best reputation. Yet the lawyers were very persuasive and assured Jose that finances wouldn't be a problem when it came to funding a project such as this. Find the space, and the money would be an afterthought. FYI, when someone tells you money is no issue, be sure that it will be. Of course, it was. One backer fell out completely and the other put together a business proposal that would leave Jose and Philippe working for them for the next ten years with little to show for it. No matter, Jose and Philippe powered on. They felt strongly enough about the success of the project that they took the cash flow from Les Halles and made it work on their own. A huge gamble on the unknown. No risk, no reward.

Le Marais, the literal translation of which is *the marsh* or *swamp*, is a district of Paris on the right side of the Seine River. It is known not only for its population of artists, but for its strong Jewish community. Now that a name

was chosen, a location soon followed. But those were the easy parts. The next challenge was learning the rules behind kosher cooking and more importantly, getting to understand the differences between the needs of a kosher guest and a non-kosher guest. As Jose found out right away, there really wasn't any difference. Kosher guests came into the restaurant demanding the same thing that all restaurant customers demanded: the best quality product and reliable service, all at a reasonable price. This is what Jose did well for his whole career, why would now be any different? He made sure that all of the steaks that left the kitchen were never fresh, but always aged. So when your mom comes in and asks, "Is it fresh?" we proudly say no. The cuts that could hold up to dry aging were aged for four weeks and the others were wet aged for the same period. Suddenly, being an observant Jew no longer meant having to put up with chewy meat and sub-par food. So Jose and his butcher got their mitts on a prime rib, looked it over, and then came up with an idea. Why not remove the cap of the rib eye and then use the center as a kosher version of a fillet (our tournedos). Now being left with the beef cap, they grilled that off and to their surprise – a great steak! Thus came the name La Surprise. Le Marais also had to specialize in the classic French dishes that we all loved. Beef bourguignon, coq au vin, duck confit, house-made fresh and dry sausages, as well as pâtés and rillettes from the butcher shop. Jose's culinary plan for the world domination of kosher food along with a primo location in the heart of Times Square hummed along just as they had hoped it would. Then in 2004, Jose and Philippe dissolved their partnership, with Philippe keeping Les Halles and Jose staying with Le Marais.

However, something was missing. A spark, a talent, an obnoxious yet handsome chef who could wrangle a motley crew of a staff and put them on the right track to greatness. (Can you guess who's writing this?) I really want to paint a romantic story of how I got involved, but there just isn't one. At the time I was the executive chef of another kosher restaurant in NYC by the name of Levana. I wasn't thrilled with my situation and began poking around the city to see what was available. I responded to an ad in the New York Times and sent in a résumé. Usually a massive waste of time, yet 10 minutes after faxing it out, the phone rang. I spoke with Patricia Thieffery, the real boss of Le Marais, sorry Jose, whom I now refer to as mommy, to set up an interview. I met with Jose twice, and that was that. I started on Monday. And as they say, the rest is history. I do have lots more to say on the subject, but I need to save something for the next book. Tentatively titled Shabbos Goy. Possibly Tuesdays with Moishe, we'll see.

Mark Hennessey
Executive Chef, Le Marais
March 2015

Jose Meirelles, owner, Le Marais

Mark Hennessey, executive chef, Le Marais

The Butcher

An integral part of Jose's plan to open Le Marais was to have a fully functional and self-sufficient butcher department. First and foremost, to be able to control how the meat is stored, aged, and portioned is vital to the game plan of giving our guests the best possible beef. Secondly, and of equal importance, doing everything in-house and utilizing every inch of meat that we purchase allows us to keep our operational costs as low as possible and in turn keep our menu prices as low as possible. The scraps of meat and fat that are the natural byproduct of portioning meat are of equal importance to us as is the eye of the rib. This is when having a true, old-school butcher really pays off.

What Le Marais needed was an old-school butcher who was skilled in French butchering and was also well versed in taking the beef, veal, lamb, and chicken leftovers and making magic with them. Knowing what I knew about the French and their butchers, this was not a task for those with a weak constitution. When I closed my eyes and tried to envision the right man for the role, I pictured Lenny from *Of Mice and Men*, with a French accent and a large knife. In comes Dominique. He has been the butcher at Le Marais from the day it opened. Dominique has what I would call a "unique" personality. May God help the person who calls him to place a butcher's order on a bad cell connection. Yikes! It goes without saying that over the years, Dominique has routinely tangled with the owner, chef, maître d', and many a customer. None of it of his own doing of course. I have had many pet names for him, none of which is appropriate for publishing. That being said, he is the best at what he does and has firmly stamped his impression into the history of Le Marais. We have found a way to work together to make great things happen and continue to create new products, like an awesome smoked veal bacon, and will do so until Jose shows us the door.

Sauces

As we were putting together the basic framework of what we wanted this book to be for the reader, Jose had a very interesting thought about the sauce section. In French cooking, and really all cooking, sauces play a vital role. Their flavors bring together all of the elements of the dish. So then why is the section on sauces always relegated to the back of the book?

When I was a student at the Culinary Institute of America, the first kitchen that you entered was the skills kitchen. The basics of knife cuts, sautéing, and most importantly, stock and sauce making. A chef who can't make a great sauce is, in fact, not a chef. Whether that sauce is a classic like a Sauce Robert, or something more contemporary like a citrus–mustard seed emulsion, great sauces in a restaurant demand the highest of technical expertise. Certainly, you aren't going to become a *saucier* just by reading this section, but you can pick up enough of the basics to impress the hell out of your dinner guests.

Rich Brown Veal Stock/Sauce Espagnole

Makes approximately 1½ quarts

You need to start with a good stock. Here is the rich veal stock that we use as a base for sauces at Le Marais, including our two most popular – the shallot sauce and the peppercorn sauce.

Here is what separates the men from the boys and the pros from the home cooks: the quality of the stock. We take it one step further by using veal shanks; they are loaded with natural gelatin and make for a richer sauce. I will concede that making a stock of this caliber at home is a major pain. Not to mention that you will need the storage space in a freezer for your supply of the dark brown liquid gold. Whether you make it or not is up to you, but a bouillon cube is not a substitute, and shame on you for even thinking that it is!

3 pounds meaty veal bones

1 small Spanish onion, peeled and coarsely diced

1 small carrot, peeled and coarsely chopped

2 ribs celery, coarsely chopped

2 cloves garlic, peeled

3 tablespoons tomato paste

½ cup instant flour

1 cup dry red wine, such as cabernet sauvignon

Preheat the oven to 400°F. Place the bones in a 17 by 12-inch roasting pan and roast them in the oven until they are deep brown in color and smell stupidly good. This should take about 25 to 30 minutes. Turn the bones occasionally to ensure even browning on all sides. When ready, remove the pan from the oven and set aside.

Place a 6-quart stockpot on the stovetop over medium heat and carefully pour in all the fat from the bottom of the roasting pan. Add the onion, carrots, celery, and garlic and cook until browned, about 12 minutes. Stir in the tomato paste and cook for an additional four minutes. Sprinkle the flour over the vegetables and mix well with a large spoon so that all of the vegetables are well coated. Add the red wine to the pot to deglaze the bottom of the pan. Use a wooden spoon to scrape up all of the bits and nubbins on the bottom of the pot. Add approximately 2½ quarts of water and bring everything to a rolling boil. Add the roasted bones to the pot, lower the temperature on the stovetop to very low heat, and simmer for 12 hours.

When ready, strain the stock into a large, clean bowl placed over an ice bath, and use a ladle to remove as much of the fat from the top of the stock as possible. When the stock is cold to the touch, portion the stock into smaller containers and freeze them for later use for up to two months.

Basic Blond Chicken Stock

Makes 1 quart

A pale stock made of either chicken, veal, or fish is also in every saucier's par stock. I'm sure that all of you have been making a chicken stock at home for forever and a day and surely don't need me to give you a recipe for one. But just in case, here it is.

2 pounds fresh chicken bones
1 large Spanish onion, peeled and coarsely chopped

1 small carrot, peeled and coarsely chopped
2 ribs celery, coarsely chopped

Place a 3-quart stockpot on the stovetop over medium heat. Add all of the ingredients to the pot and cover with 2 quarts of cold water. Bring everything slowly to a boil, then lower the temperature on the stovetop to low heat and bring the mixture down to a simmer. The stock should simmer slowly for five hours: it takes this long to coax all of the flavor and gelatin out of the bones. Along the way, you will need to skim off any scum or impurities from the surface of the simmering stock.

When ready, strain the stock into a large, clean bowl placed over an ice bath, and use a ladle to remove as much of the fat from the top of the stock as possible. When the stock is cold to the touch, portion the stock into smaller containers and freeze them for later use for up to two months.

At this point your freezer should be look like a Chinese restaurant, filled with those plastic quart containers.

Mother Sauces

The French have what are called the Grand Sauces, or as most chefs call them, the Mother Sauces. Simply put, they are base sauces that are adapted in countless number of ways, to create numerous offspring sauces. Let's now go over the five mother sauces, and just how to turn them into the sauces that you can recreate at home.

The mother sauces are the following:

- Demi-glace
- Velouté
- Hollandaise
- Tomato sauce
- Béchamel

I'm going to throw in one more sauce, Escoffier and Fernand Point be damned: the Vinaigrette. In any contemporary kitchen, the vinaigrette is used as a complementary sauce for every protein and vegetable imaginable. I believe that if Escoffier were alive today, he would agree with me. He would also be over 160 years old and fairly gross.

Before making a sauce, give some thought as to what its function on the plate will be and which sauce will work with which dish. For example, if you're making a chicken dish and want to make an accompanying mushroom sauce, a velouté will be the most logical choice because the base of the velouté is made with chicken stock. That doesn't mean that any of the other mother-sauce bases won't work, because they will; it's just a question of what the best complement is for a particular dish.

Demi-Glace

Makes 1 quart

A true demi-glace is made by combining a brown stock with a sauce Espagnole and reducing them down by ½. But there's no point in making a brown stock and a sauce Espagnole if you're really only going to need one of them.

2½ quarts Rich Brown Veal Stock/Sauce Espagnole (page 2)

Place a 4-quart saucepan on the stovetop over medium heat and add the stock. Cook until the stock has reduced by slightly less than half, to about one quart. Strain the sauce through cheesecloth or a fine mesh strainer and into a clean bowl to be used as needed.

Demi-glace is best used the day that it is made. However, it can be stored in an airtight container in the refrigerator for up to three days.

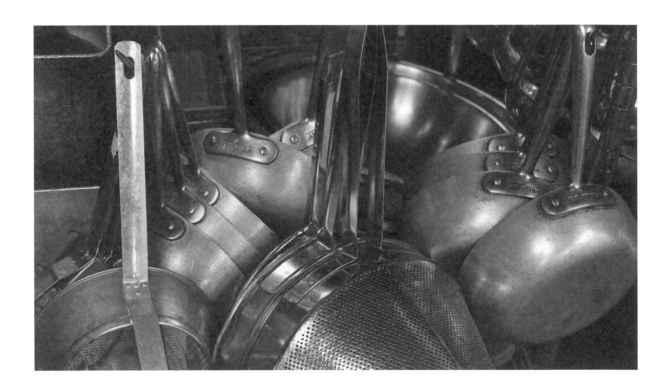

LE MARAIS DEMI-GLACE SAUCE
VARIATION 1 LE MARAIS AU POIVRE SAUCE

MAKES 1 QUART

A classic au poivre sauce uses butter and heavy cream. Delicious, but not gonna work here. So, here is what we make. You should not add all of the pepper in the recipe all at once; do it in ¼ increments so that you can adjust the level of pepperiness to your taste.

2 tablespoons extra virgin olive oil

1 small shallot, peeled and sliced

2 cloves garlic, peeled and sliced

1 teaspoon tomato paste

¼ cup instant flour

1 small bunch thyme, tied together with string

1 fresh bay leaf

1 cup Demi-Glace (page 6)

¼ cup cognac

Salt

1 tablespoon coarsely ground black pepper

Place a 3-quart saucepot on the stovetop over medium heat and add the oil, shallots, and garlic. Cook, stirring the shallots occasionally, until they turn a rich brown color. Be careful, you don't want them to burn. Once all of the shallots have caramelized, stir in the tomato paste and cook for another five minutes. Sprinkle the flour over the vegetables and mix well with a large spoon so that all of the vegetables are well coated. Cook for another two minutes, then add the thyme, bay leaf, and demi-glace.

Remove the pan from the stovetop and add the cognac. Carefully put the pan back on the stovetop over medium heat. If you are on a gas stovetop, the cognac may ignite so you want to be sure you do not stand directly over the pan. Allow the sauce to cook until the flame has gone out. It's ok if the cognac does not catch fire and burn; the alcohol will still cook off. Raise the temperature on the stovetop to high heat and bring the sauce up to a boil. Lower the temperature on the stovetop back down to medium heat and cook until the sauce is thick enough to coat the back of a spoon.

Strain the sauce through a fine mesh sieve and into a clean 2-quart saucepan, discarding the solids. Season the sauce with salt, and place the saucepan on the stovetop over medium heat and bring back to a simmer. Stir in the black pepper ½ teaspoon at a time, and let the sauce simmer for a minute before tasting. Continue to add pepper until your desired level of spice has been reached.

Use the sauce immediately or cool down over an ice bath and store in the refrigerator for up to four days or in the freezer for up to two weeks.

Le Marais Demi-Glace Sauce
Variation 2 Le Marais Shallot Sauce

Makes approximately 1 quart

2 tablespoons extra virgin olive oil

1 cup sliced shallots

2 cloves garlic, peeled and sliced

1 teaspoon tomato paste

½ cup instant flour

½ (750-ml) bottle big red
wine, such as Bordeaux

1 small bunch thyme, tied
together with kitchen twine

1 fresh bay leaf

1 quart Demi-Glace
(page 6)

Salt and freshly ground
black pepper

Place a 3-quart saucepot on the stovetop over medium heat and add the oil, shallots, and garlic. Cook, stirring the shallots occasionally, until they turn a rich brown color. Be careful, you don't want them to burn. Once all of the shallots have caramelized, stir in the tomato paste and cook for another five minutes. Sprinkle the flour over the vegetables and mix well with a large spoon so that all of the vegetables are well coated. Cook for another two minutes and add the red wine. Cook until the liquid has reduced by about one-fourth. Stir in the thyme, bay leaf, and demi-glace. Raise the temperature on the stovetop to medium-high heat and bring the mixture up to a boil. Cook until the sauce is thick enough to coat the back of a spoon. Season the sauce with salt and pepper.

Use the sauce immediately or cool down over an ice bath and store in the refrigerator for up to five days or in the freezer for up to two weeks.

VELOUTÉ

MAKES 2 CUPS

A velouté is a sauce that is made with a white stock (chicken, veal, or fish) and is thickened with a roux. The roux is the flour-and-oil mixture that is in the recipe below.

2 cups white stock (page 3)

Pale roux:

1 tablespoon either peanut oil, vegetable oil, or unsalted margarine, or unsalted butter if using fish

2 tablespoons all-purpose flour
Salt and white pepper

Place a 2-quart saucepan on the stovetop over low heat and add the stock. Bring to a simmer while you are making your roux.

TO MAKE THE ROUX: Place a 1-quart saucepan on the stovetop over medium-low heat and add the oil. Add the flour all at once, and use a wooden spoon or whisk to stir/whisk the roux constantly while cooking to a pale, ivory color; this should take anywhere from six to nine minutes.

While whisking, gradually add the roux to the simmering stock. Keep whisking until all of the roux has been added and the stock is smooth. Raise the temperature on the stovetop to medium or medium-high heat and bring the stock to a full boil.

Then lower the temperature on the stovetop to low heat and bring the sauce down to a low simmer. The sauce will need to simmer for about 35 to 45 minutes. Be sure to occasionally whisk the sauce, and watch the heat. If the temperature is up too high, the sauce will scorch on the bottom. Along the way, you will need to skim off any scum or impurities from the surface of the simmering stock.

When ready, strain the sauce through a cheesecloth or a fine mesh sieve, unless you like your sauces just like mom's, extra lumpy please.

Use the sauce immediately or cool down over an ice bath and store in the refrigerator for up to four days.

HOLLANDAISE

MAKES APPROXIMATELY 2 CUPS

Unlike the previous two mother sauces, a hollandaise is an emulsion sauce. An emulsion is formed when one substance is suspended into another. In this case, it is melted margarine or butter that is suspended into slightly cooked egg yolks. It is a fragile sauce to make and to hold. However, unlike the other mother sauces, it is prepared in one fell swoop and doesn't require a stock to be made in advance. Chances are that your first attempt to make this will be a disaster. You will more than likely either scramble the eggs or not whisk enough to get the emulsion done correctly. No worries, we've all done it. Once you do get it right, it will be an invaluable weapon in your arsenal against the evils of dinner parties.

Since we're a kosher meat restaurant, we use margarine for this sauce. Yet these sauces are amazing with fish, giving you a valid reason to make this using butter. A very high quality of butter is recommended for this, since it will be the predominant flavor.

4 large egg yolks
2 tablespoons freshly
squeezed lemon juice

8 tablespoons (1 stick / ½ cup) unsalted
margarine or butter, melted and warm
Salt and white pepper

Make a water bath by placing a 2-quart saucepan on the stovetop over low heat and filling half full with water. Bring the water to a boil, then lower the temperature on the stovetop to low heat and let the water simmer until ready to use.

Place the egg yolks and lemon juice in a non-reactive bowl and whisk vigorously by hand until the eggs have thickened and doubled in volume.

Place the bowl with the eggs over the simmering water and continue to whisk.

[SIDENOTE: Here are some tips when making hollandaise over a water bath: First, make sure the bottom of the bowl does not touch the water in the pan. If it does, discard some of the water as needed. Next, periodically remove the bowl from the water bath to prevent the eggs from becoming too hot and overcooking or scrambling.]

While whisking, slowly drizzle the warm margarine into the eggs. If you want, you can use a handheld immersion blender instead of a whisk. As the margarine is added, the sauce should thicken and then double in volume. Remove the bowl from the water bath and season the sauce with salt and pepper.

If not using right away, you can hold the sauce in a thermos for up to two hours to keep it warm until ready to use. Simply pour the hollandaise out when you are ready to serve.

Le Marais Hollandaise Variation Béarnaise

⅔ cups white wine, such as chardonnay

1 shallot, peeled and minced

4 sprigs tarragon, leaves only, finely chopped, divided

4 large egg yolks

8 tablespoons (1 stick / ½ cup) unsalted margarine or butter

Salt and white pepper

Place a 2-quart saucepan on the stovetop over medium heat. Add the wine, shallots, and half of the tarragon and bring to a boil. Cook, boiling, until all of the liquid has evaporated. Remove from the heat and set aside until ready to use.

Make a water bath by placing a 2-quart saucepan on the stovetop over medium heat and filling half full with water. Bring the water to a boil, then lower the temperature on the stovetop to low and let the water simmer until ready to use.

Place the egg yolks and warm shallot reduction in a non-reactive bowl and whisk vigorously by hand until the eggs have thickened and doubled in volume. See a trend here? Follow the same procedure as when making a hollandaise sauce (see page 10). At the end, fold in the remaining tarragon.

If not using right away, you can hold the sauce in a thermos for up to two hours to keep it warm until ready to use. Simply pour the Béarnaise out when you are ready to serve.

TOMATO SAUCE

MAKES 2 QUARTS

Yes, this is a classic French mother sauce, not just a way to finish off your rigatoni. I have to believe that if there were a committee formed to reevaluate the mother sauces this one may not make the list and would instead be replaced by the vinaigrette. In any case, this is not a marinara sauce, but a very good base sauce that can be used as a standalone sauce or as a base for a braise.

2 tablespoons extra virgin olive oil	½ cup chicken stock (see page 3)
½ small carrot, peeled and cut into ½-inch dice	½ cup tomato paste
½ small Spanish onion, peeled and cut into ½-inch dice	1 pound roasted chicken bones
1 clove garlic, peeled and sliced	1 fresh bay leaf
1 teaspoon all-purpose flour	1 small bunch thyme
1 (28-ounce) can whole plum tomatoes, strained and cut into ½-inch dice	Salt and freshly ground black pepper

Place a 4-quart saucepot on the stovetop over medium heat and add the oil. Add the carrots, onion, and garlic and cook gently until all of the vegetables have softened, about eight minutes. Sprinkle the flour over the vegetables and mix well with a large spoon so that all of the vegetables are well coated, and cook for an additional five minutes.

Stir in the tomatoes, chicken stock, tomato paste, chicken bones, bay leaf, and the thyme. Lower the temperature on the stovetop to low heat and simmer the sauce for about 1½ to two hours, until the sauce has reduced by about one-third.

Use tongs or a slotted spoon to remove the chicken bones and the bay leaf and discard them. Purée the remaining sauce in the container of an electric blender until very smooth. Season with salt and pepper.

Use the sauce immediately or cool down over an ice bath and store in the refrigerator for up to five days or in the freezer for up to two months.

[SIDENOTE: Use the sauce as a braising liquid for veal or chicken.]

[SIDENOTE: A Spanish tomato sauce, a tomato sauce derivative, is made by adding sautéed mushrooms, green peppers, onions, and garlic to a simmering tomato sauce.]

BÉCHAMEL

MAKES 1 QUART

The béchamel is a white sauce that is made by thickening milk with a pale roux and simmering it with aromatics. In modern America, as far as I know, the place that you would see a béchamel most nowadays is as the base for a cheese sauce for mac and cheese. It does make for a luxuriously creamy sauce for salmon, halibut, or any other fish. Mix a little béchamel with some of the tomato sauce, and you've got yourself an amazing pasta sauce. This one, we do not make at Le Marais. Before you even ask, no, a parve version of this isn't feasible by using nondairy substitutes such as soy milk. With this it's dairy or bust.

2 teaspoons unsalted butter

1 small onion, peeled and cut into ¼-inch dice

1 quart whole milk

2 sprigs thyme

½ fresh bay leaf

2 recipes pale roux (page 9), heated and kept warm on the stovetop

½ teaspoon freshly grated nutmeg

Place a 2-quart saucepan on the stovetop over medium heat and add the butter. Add the onion and cook until soft and translucent. Add the milk, thyme, and the bay leaf, and then bring everything to a boil. Whisking constantly, slowly add the roux until fully incorporated. Bring the mixture to a boil, continuously whisking until completely smooth and lump free.

Lower the temperature on the stovetop to low heat and bring the sauce to a slow simmer. Because of the milk and the flour, scorching is a real concern here. Be sure that the heat is truly on a low simmer. Skim the top of the sauce to remove any foam or impurities and simmer for at least 30 minutes and for up to as long as 60 minutes. Add the grated nutmeg at the end and strain the sauce through cheesecloth or a fine mesh sieve and into a clean bowl.

This sauce is best if used immediately, or cool down over an ice bath and store in the refrigerator for up to three days.

Variations:

Dijon Mustard Sauce

Whisk in ½ cup of high quality Dijon mustard to the finished béchamel.

Mornay Sauce

½ cup grated Gruyère cheese

½ cup grated parmesan cheese

1 pint freshly made, warm béchamel sauce

Fold the cheese into the sauce until fully incorporated and smooth.

Vinaigrettes

When the Mother Sauce committee meets, I'm assuming that it will be the culinary version of the Illuminati and I will also assume that I will neither be invited nor even made aware of its existence. But if I were invited, I would hereby declare that tomato sauce is no longer a mother sauce and that the vinaigrette will now take its place. The vinaigrette is the epitome of modern cookery: it's light and crisp, and you are easily able to identify all of the culprits involved.

Vinaigrettes are also extraordinarily versatile. You can change the acid, the oil, the aromatics, the herbs, add sweetness, spices, whatever. Also, because it's an emulsion sauce, it benefits from the use of machinery. A blender works wonders on getting vinaigrettes to come together. They can be used to sauce beef, chicken, vegetables, salads, and fish. Also, if they are emulsified properly, they can be held stable in the refrigerator.

BASIC VINAIGRETTE

Mix up the oils, vinegars, or juices of your choice to create your own recipes. Vinaigrettes can be made up to five days in advance and stored in the refrigerator until ready to use.

½ cup vinegar or freshly squeezed citrus juice of your choice

Salt and freshly ground pepper

½ teaspoon Dijon mustard

1 tablespoon freshly chopped herbs, such as parsley, tarragon, or chives

1½ cups oil of your choice

Place the vinegar, salt, pepper, mustard, and herbs in the container of an electric blender. Cover the container with the lid. With the blender running, slowly drizzle in the oil until fully incorporated. If the consistency of the vinaigrette is too thick for your liking, you can thin it with a little water before using.

LE MARAIS VINAIGRETTE

½ small shallot, peeled

1 clove garlic, peeled

1 small bunch flat leaf (Italian) parsley, freshly chopped

2 tablespoons honey

¼ cup Dijon mustard

1 cup balsamic vinegar

1½ cups extra virgin olive oil

1½ cups peanut or vegetable oil

Salt and freshly ground black pepper

Place the shallot, garlic, parsley, honey, mustard, and vinegar in the container of an electric blender. Cover the container with the lid. With the blender running, slowly drizzle in the oil until fully incorporated. Season the vinaigrette with the salt and pepper. If the consistency of the vinaigrette is too thick for your liking, you can thin it with a little water before using.

FRESH MAYONNAISE

MAKES 1¼ CUPS

I don't know who is in charge of things like this, but it's time for the list of mother sauces to be expanded. I've put in the calls to the culinary Illuminati of Boulud, Keller and Vongerichten. Predictably, no return calls to the likes of me.

A mayonnaise is ultra-versatile. It's the base for a tartar sauce, aioli, and a million other creamy sauces. Here is the base recipe for a fresh mayo. Whisk in fresh herbs, spices, vegetable purées, or hot sauces to create your own sauces. To answer the obvious question, yes, it is much better than prepared mayos and it is worth the extra effort.

> 2 large egg yolks
> 1 teaspoon Dijon mustard
> 4 teaspoons lemon juice or rice wine vinegar
> 1 cup peanut oil or sunflower oil
> Kosher salt and white pepper

Place the egg yolks, mustard, and lemon juice in the bowl of a food processor fitted with the blade attachment and blend until well incorporated.

With the processor running, slowly drizzle in the oil until fully incorporated, and the mixture is thick and emulsified.

Once all of the oil has been added, season the mayonnaise with the salt and white pepper to your liking.

Keep in mind that if you are going to flavor the mayonnaise, go easy with the seasoning. You should adjust the seasoning after you add any other flavor.

Freshly made mayonnaise can be stored in the refrigerator, covered, for up to two weeks.

Salads

Whether or not you buy this book, receive it as a gift, or pull it off a library shelf or out of a discount bin at the local dollar store, I'm guessing that of all of the things that you are looking for in here, the salad section is on the bottom of your list. On that note, as far as I am concerned, the salad section should be in the back of the book. Are any of you looking through a steak house cookbook and thinking, "Hmmm, just how do they make that tomato/watermelon salad?" If you're that person, then this is for you. As a matter of fact, since nobody is reading this, this would be a great place for me to rant on about the things that drive me nuts. I won't, but I should. Vegetarians, the French, people who eat an entire plate of food only to complain that they don't like it and want something else, and people who eat half a candy bar and then put the rest into the refrigerator. Just a little rant. Once again, I lied.

Summer Jicama Slaw

Serves 8

The crunchy acidity that this provides is ideal with your warm weather BBQ as well as a foil for any rich, fatty meat dish.

Vinaigrette:

½ cup freshly squeezed lime juice

2 tablespoons apple cider vinegar

2 tablespoons honey

1 teaspoon caraway seeds

½ cup extra virgin olive oil

Salt and freshly ground
black pepper

Slaw:

1 large jicama, peeled and thinly
cut into 2-inch lengths

½ cup Napa cabbage, shredded

2 medium-sized carrots, peeled and
thinly cut into 2-inch lengths

3 scallions, white and green
parts, chopped

¼ cup freshly chopped cilantro or basil

Place the lime juice, vinegar, honey, caraway seeds, and oil in bowl and whisk to combine. Season with salt and pepper.

Place the jicama, cabbage, carrots, scallions, and herbs in a large bowl. Toss with the dressing, and then taste for seasoning.

Let the salad sit at room temperature for about 15 minutes before serving to allow time for the slaw to fully absorb some of the dressing.

Charred Vidalia Onion Salad

Serves 8

Vinaigrette:

¼ cup balsamic vinegar

2 tablespoons Dijon mustard

¾ cups extra virgin olive oil

Salt and freshly ground black pepper

Onions:

4 medium-sized Vidalia onions,
peeled and cut into ½-inch slices

Salt and freshly ground black pepper

2 tablespoons extra virgin olive oil

2 tablespoons balsamic vinegar

To serve:

1 tablespoon freshly chopped mint

1 tablespoon freshly chopped basil

2 cups mixed colored cherry tomatoes,
rinsed, stemmed and halved

2 cups loosely packed
arugula leaves, rinsed

TO MAKE THE VINAIGRETTE: Place the vinegar and mustard in a bowl and whisk together to combine. While whisking, slowly drizzle in the oil to form an emulsion. You can also do this in the container of an electric blender (just be sure to rinse out the margaritas!). Season with salt and pepper and set aside until ready to use.

TO MAKE THE ONIONS: Preheat and season the grill. If using a gas grill, turn the heat up to medium high. Next, clean the grates with a grill brush, being sure to remove any residue from your previous day's grilling. Fold a clean rag or a bunch of paper towels into a thick cylinder shape. Use clean vegetable oil and drizzle some of the oil onto the towel cylinder. Then grab the towel with a pair of tongs and run it up and down the length of the grates until all of the grates are clean.

Season the onion slices with salt and pepper. Drizzle the slices with oil and vinegar.

Place the onions in a single layer on the grill. Depending on the size of your grill, you may need to grill the onions in batches. Once on the hot grill, the onions should begin to caramelize in about three minutes. Don't flip or fiddle with the onions, let them be. Once they have caramelized, use a spatula and flip them over. Grill for another three to four minutes. They should be well caramelized on both sides and soft.

TO SERVE: While still warm from the grill, toss the onions with the herbs, cherry tomatoes, arugula, and the vinaigrette. Taste the tossed salad and season with salt and pepper. Serve immediately.

Heirloom Tomato and Watermelon Salad

I may be the only chef who will publicly say the following: Farm to table, local, and sustainable have become nothing more than catch words for farmers to market their own products. Don't get me wrong – in a perfect world, this is how it should be. To be honest, if I could get perfect strawberries and tomatoes in the heart of February that were grown on the dark side of the moon out of a baboon's bright red backside, I would buy it, eat it, and sell it. But for the time being, the best tomatoes and melons are available in the late summer and that's when you should take advantage of these beautiful products and this beautifully simple salad.

4 large, fresh, ripe heirloom tomatoes, rinsed and cored

1 pound watermelon flesh, seeded and cut into ½-inch dice

1 bunch basil leaves

1 cup toasted pine nuts

Juice of 2 lemons

2 tablespoons extra virgin olive oil

Coarse sea salt

Freshly ground black pepper

Cut the tomatoes into wedges. Place the tomato wedges, watermelon, basil, and pine nuts in a bowl and toss with the lemon juice and oil. Season well with salt and pepper.

When ready to plate and serve, tap into your inner artist and add an additional drizzle of olive oil over the entire plate. This salad is best when made immediately before serving.

Salad of Roasted Pears, Watercress, and Toasted Pecans

Serves 8

This is a great starter salad, especially if you are making a dairy meal. Add some crumbled goat cheese or gorgonzola for richness.

Toasted pecans:

2 cups shelled pecan halves

Pears:

4 firm Anjou pears, halved lengthwise and cored

Salt and freshly ground pepper

2 tablespoons (¼ stick / ⅛ cup) unsalted margarine

½ cup honey

6 sprigs thyme

Vinaigrette:

½ cup red wine vinegar

2 small shallots, peeled and minced

2 tablespoons Dijon mustard

1½ cups peanut or grape seed oil

Salt and freshly ground black pepper

To serve:

4 cups watercress, rinsed and stemmed

Preheat the oven to 375°F.

TO MAKE THE PECANS: Place the pecans on a clean baking sheet and toast in the oven for about seven to eight minutes. You want them to take on a slightly dark appearance. Toasting the pecans will give them a richer, more complex flavor.

TO MAKE THE PEARS: Season the pears on all sides with salt and pepper. Place an ovenproof, 10-inch skillet on the stovetop over medium heat and add the margarine. Add the pears, cut side down, and cook until nicely browned. Add the honey and the thyme.

Place the pan in the oven and bake for about 10 to 12 minutes. The time will vary based on the ripeness of the pears. They are ready when a small knife inserted into the center of a pear can be removed without any resistance. If the pears are not as caramelized in color as you would like, place the pan back on the stovetop over medium-high heat and brown to your desired color.

TO MAKE THE VINAIGRETTE: Place the vinegar, shallots, and mustard in a bowl and whisk to combine. While whisking, slowly drizzle in the oil until fully incorporated. The resulting vinaigrette should be emulsified and creamy, but if not, that's fine. In this salad it will work just as well as long as the ingredients are well combined. Season with salt and pepper.

TO SERVE: Dress the watercress with enough vinaigrette to generously coat, and divide evenly among eight plates. Slice each pear half in half again lengthwise and serve half a pear per plate. Alternately you can cut each pear half into slices.

Sprinkle the salad with the toasted pecans.

FRISÉE AUX LARDONS

SERVES 8

If I have to eat a salad – and my wife insists that I do on occasion – then it better damn well have bacon. You need a thick slab of bacon to pull this off, thin slices of the "facon" that is sold at kosher butcher counters just ain't gonna cut the mustard. It's a good thing that I make just such a product at Le Marais.

Croutons:

4 (¾-inch-thick) slices brioche or challah bread, cut into ¾-inch cubes

3 tablespoons extra virgin olive oil, plus extra for greasing the pan

Salt and freshly ground black pepper

Lardons:

12 ounces smoked veal bacon

2 tablespoons extra virgin olive oil

1 small shallot, peeled and minced

3 tablespoons red wine vinegar

Poached eggs:

8 large eggs

3 drops white vinegar

To serve:

3 heads frisée, rinsed and stemmed

Salt and freshly ground black pepper

TO MAKE THE CROUTONS: Preheat the oven to 350°F. Lightly oil a clean baking sheet and set aside until ready to use.

Place the bread and oil in a large bowl and toss to combine. Season with salt and pepper. Spread the cubes onto the prepared baking sheet and bake in the oven for about 13 minutes, or until all of the bread is brown and toasted. Remove from the oven and set aside until ready to use.

TO MAKE THE LARDONS: Cut the bacon into ¼-inch-thick slices. Stack the slices on top of each other and then cut them into ¼-inch lengths, or lardons.

Place an 8-inch skillet on the stovetop over medium heat and add the oil. Add the lardons and cook until browned on all sides. Add the shallots and cook for an additional two minutes. Stir in the vinegar to

deglaze the pan. Remove the pan from the stovetop and set aside while you poach the eggs.

TO POACH THE EGGS: Place a 4-quart saucepan on the stovetop over medium heat and fill half full with water. Stir in the white vinegar and bring to a low simmer. Break one egg into a teacup. Slide the egg into the simmering liquid and use a slotted spoon to immediately but gently swirl the egg white clockwise around the yolk. (If you are doing this correctly, the egg will become oval shaped with the yolk completely covered by the egg white.) Repeat with the remaining 3 eggs. Simmer the eggs about three minutes apiece for runny yolks. Use a slotted spoon to carefully transfer the poached eggs to the saucepan of warm water.

If the bacon has cooled down, place the pan back

on the stovetop over medium heat and cook just long enough to rewarm the bacon. Place the frisée, croutons, and bacon mixture in a bowl and toss to combine.

Divide the salad evenly among eight plates, and top each with what is hopefully a perfectly poached egg. Season the entire salad with freshly cracked black pepper.

CAESAR SALAD WITH ANCHOVY VINAIGRETTE AND ROSEMARY FLATBREAD

Here's the dilemma: a classic Caesar salad is a favorite, but a prime ingredient is the parmesan in the dressing. My theory has always been not to try to replace a great ingredient with a subpar one and I won't do it here. This works very well but who are we kidding, it's not the same. Don't be freaked out by the raw egg yolk, research shows that only about 1 of 20,000 eggs are contaminated with salmonella. If it bothers you that much, you can buy pasteurized egg yolks.

Flatbread:

½ cup bread flour, plus extra for dusting

½ cup finely ground corn meal

Pinch salt

Pinch freshly ground black pepper

½ cup warm water

3 sprigs rosemary, leaves only, coarsely chopped

Anchovy vinaigrette:

1 large egg yolk

3 tablespoons freshly squeezed lemon juice

1 teaspoon minced garlic

2 anchovy fillets, left whole

1½ tablespoons Dijon mustard

Salt and freshly ground black pepper

¾ cup peanut or olive oil

To serve:

1 head romaine lettuce, rinsed and coarsely chopped

TO MAKE THE FLATBREAD: Preheat the oven to 400°F. Place a clean, flat baking sheet in the oven to preheat. If you have room for multiple baking sheets, this will speed up the process as the recipe makes six flatbreads.

Place the flour, corn meal, rosemary, salt and pepper in a large bowl and mix to combine. Drizzle in the water in several additions while mixing together with by hand to form a firm, non-sticky dough.

Lightly dust a clean work surface with flour and use a knife to cut the dough into six pieces. Working one piece of dough at a time, roll out the dough as thinly as possible; the thinner the dough, the crispier the flatbread will be. Oval or round, the shape is really up to you. Repeat with the remaining dough until you have six pieces rolled out and ready to bake.

Carefully remove the hot baking sheets from the oven, flip them over and lay one or two pieces of the rolled out dough onto the backside of each of the baking sheets, leaving space in between if you are baking multiple pieces. Put the baking sheets back into the hot oven, dough side up of course, and bake the dough for between eight to 10 minutes, or until the flatbread is lightly browned and crisp. Remove the flatbread from the oven and cool on a clean towel. The flatbread will fully crisp up as it cools.

TO MAKE THE VINAIGRETTE: Place the egg yolk, lemon juice, garlic, anchovies, mustard, salt and pepper in a bowl and whisk well to combine. While whisking, slowly drizzle in the oil. Continue whisking until all of the oil has been fully incorporated and the vinaigrette is smooth and creamy. Store the vinaigrette, covered, in the refrigerator until ready to use or for up to one week.

TO SERVE: Place the romaine lettuce in a large salad bowl, dress with as much vinaigrette as you like, and toss together until very well combined. Break the flatbread into large, uneven pieces and arrange them on the serving plates alongside the dressed greens.

Tuna Niçoise Salad

SERVES 8

The niçoise salad originated in Nice, France. The idea is simple: take fresh local produce, local tuna, and crisp lettuce to form a refreshing salad. Whereas I always prefer fresh tuna, if you can find a quality canned tuna that could be a good substitute. When I say quality tuna, I don't mean the standard stuff on your supermarket shelves. The French, Spaniards, and Portuguese have some exceptionally good seafood in a can; you just have to hunt it out a little.

8 ounces fresh haricot vert, stemmed

8 fingerling Yukon Gold potatoes, scrubbed

8 (3-ounce) portions fresh Yellowfin tuna, skinned

Salt and white pepper

2 tablespoons peanut oil

2 heads butter lettuce, or any other crisp lettuce, rinsed and cored

1 pint cherry tomatoes, rinsed and stemmed

1 large red onion, peeled and thinly sliced

1½ cups pitted Niçoise or Kalamata olives

2 cups Le Marais Vinaigrette (page 16)

8 large eggs, hard-boiled and peeled (page 62)

2 (2-ounce) cans anchovies

TO MAKE THE HARICOT VERT: Place a 2-quart saucepan on the stovetop over high heat and fill half full with water. Add a generous amount of salt and bring the water to a boil. Drop the haricot vert into the water and boil for about two minutes. They should turn bright green in color and be tender to the bite. Remove the haricot vert from the hot water and immediately submerge them in a bowl of ice water to stop the cooking. When cooled all the way through, drain the beans and store in the refrigerator. The haricot vert can be prepared up to 24 hours in advance.

[SIDENOTE: Keep in mind that if you leave the beans in the cold water for too long, they will absorb the water and taste like mushy, watery beans.]

TO MAKE THE POTATOES: Place a 3-quart saucepot on the stovetop over high heat and add the potatoes. Add enough cold water to cover the potatoes and bring everything to a boil. Once the water has reached a boil, lower the temperature on the stovetop to medium heat and simmer until the potatoes are tender; they are ready when a knife inserted in the center can be removed easily. Remove the potatoes from the hot water and submerge them in a bowl of ice water to stop the cooking. When cooled, drain the potatoes and set aside until ready to use. The potatoes can be prepared up to 24 hours in advance.

If you are able to get your hands on good quality, canned tuna you can skip this next step. FYI, good quality tuna won't be on sale for $.99, nor will it have the word chicken on the label.

TO MAKE THE TUNA: You can sear the tuna on a

grill or on the stovetop. Either way, make sure the cooking surface is hot as hell when ready. Preheat the grill and season with peanut oil (see page 102) or place a nonstick, 8-inch sauté pan on the stovetop over high heat and add the oil. Season the tuna well on all sides with salt and pepper. Place the tuna onto the scorching hot cooking surface to sear, or brown. After 30 seconds, flip each piece over to sear the other side. After another 30 seconds, remove the tuna from the heat.

When ready to serve, place the lettuce leaves, haricot vert, tomatoes, onions, and olives in a large bowl and toss with the Le Marais Vinaigrette. Arrange the salad on a large platter or divide evenly among eight plates. Slice the eggs and potatoes in half lengthwise and place around the outside of the platter. Lay the anchovies over the dressed salad. Cut each piece of tuna into four or more slices and layer these over the top of the salad.

Sautéed Chicken Breast Salad with Fine Herbs, Roasted Radishes, and Pomegranate Seeds

Serves 6

Chicken:

6 boneless, skinless, chicken breasts

Salt and freshly ground black pepper

4 tablespoons extra virgin olive oil

12 whole radishes, tops cut off, halved lengthwise

½ (750-ml) bottle white wine, such as sauvignon blanc

4 sprigs thyme

Salad:

3 bunches arugula, rinsed and stemmed

4 sprigs flat leaf (Italian) parsley, leaves only

8 sprigs chervil, leaves only

1 small bunch chives, freshly chopped

2 tablespoons extra virgin olive oil

Salt and freshly ground black pepper

Seeds from ½ fresh pomegranate

2 lemons

TO MAKE THE CHICKEN: Preheat the oven to 400°F.

Place an ovenproof, 10-inch sauté pan on the stovetop over high heat and add the oil. Season the chicken breasts liberally with salt and pepper. When the pan is hot, add the chicken to the pan and sear, or brown, on all sides. You may need to sear the chicken in batches to avoid overcrowding the pan. Once all of the breasts have been seared, remove them from the pan and set aside until ready to use.

Add the radishes to the same pan and brown on all sides. Stir in the wine and the fresh thyme.

Return the chicken breasts to the pan, place the pan in the oven and roast for 10 minutes, until they are firm to the touch, yet give slightly when poked in the center. Remove the chicken and the radishes from the pan and place on a platter. Place the pan back on the stovetop over high heat and cook until the sauce has reduced down to the consistency of a glaze. Pour the glaze over the chicken breasts and allow them to rest for at least 10 minutes before slicing.

TO MAKE THE SALAD: Place the arugula and herbs in a large bowl and toss to combine. Use a micro-plane zester to zest the skin of one lemon over the salad. Squeeze both lemons and add the juice to the salad. Drizzle the salad with oil, lightly season with salt and pepper, and toss in the pomegranate seeds.

TO SERVE: Place the salad on a serving platter, top with the sliced chicken breasts and the roasted radishes, and drizzle with extra virgin olive oil.

HANGER STEAK SALAD WITH PICKLED VEGETABLES

SERVES 8

The kosher hanger steak is, at its best, a little salty. At its worst, it is so over salted that it is virtually inedible. What this dish accomplishes is that the sweetness and the acidity from the pickled vegetables perfectly mellows out the salinity in the meat.

Brine:

2 cups apple cider vinegar

2 cups water

¼ cup kosher salt

¾ cups granulated sugar

6 pink peppercorns

1 teaspoon coriander seeds

1 fresh bay leaf

4 sprigs thyme

Juice of 2 lemons

Pickled vegetables:

1 medium-sized red onion, peeled and thinly sliced

2 red bell peppers, seeded, de-ribbed, and thinly sliced into 2-inch lengths

½ pineapple, cleaned, cored, and cut into ¼-inch dice

½ head cauliflower, broken down into florets

1 medium-sized carrot, peeled and cut into 2-inch lengths

1 bunch cilantro

Steak:

8 (8-ounce) hanger steaks

Freshly ground black pepper

4 tablespoons extra virgin olive oil

To serve:

4 bunches arugula, rinsed

3 tablespoons extra virgin olive oil

TO MAKE THE BRINE: Place a 3-quart saucepan on the stovetop over high heat and add the vinegar, water, salt, sugar, peppercorns, coriander seeds, bay leaf, thyme, and lemon juice. Bring the liquid to a boil, lower the temperature on the stovetop to low heat and simmer for 15 minutes. Strain the brine through a fine mesh sieve and into a clean container, discarding the solids. Allow the brine to cool completely. Once cooled, the brine can be used immediately or stored for several days in the refrigerator.

TO PICKLE THE VEGETABLES: When ready to use, add all of the vegetables to the cooled brine and let sit, covered, for two hours in the refrigerator or for up to one week.

TO MAKE THE STEAK: Season the hanger steak with pepper (no salt!!!). Place a 10-inch sauté pan on the stovetop over high heat, get it good and hot, and add the oil. Place the steak in the pan and sear well, or brown, on both sides.

Let the steak rest for about eight minutes before you slice into it. Cut each steak on the bias into ½-inch-thick slices.

TO SERVE: Divide the arugula evenly among the plates and top with pickled vegetables. Drizzle the salad with extra virgin olive oil and artfully layer the sliced hanger steak over the top.

DUCK CONFIT SALAD

SERVES 8

The duck leg has for so many years been seen as a nuisance. If only the ducks could be bred with the breast only! All of those poor ducks rolling around in wheelchairs, no legs to assist in hitting that landing. Thankfully, the tides have shifted and the odd parts have come into fashion. This classic salad is simply awesome. The duck legs can be prepped in advance and stored in their own fat in the refrigerator for a good long time.

In the event that you can't get duck fat, don't worry – you can use the same amount of either olive oil or any other vegetable oil.

Duck confit:

8 fresh ducks legs, skin on

Salt and freshly ground black pepper

6 cloves garlic, peeled

12 sprigs thyme

4 cups duck fat, melted just to the point of being able to pour

Potatoes:

2 Russet potatoes, peeled, cut into ¼-inch dice and held at room temperature in water

2 medium-sized shallots, peeled and thinly sliced

2 cloves garlic, peeled and thinly sliced

2 teaspoons Le Marais Vinaigrette (page 16)

To serve:

3 heads frisée, rinsed

Le Marais Vinaigrette (page 16)

1 small bunch flat leaf (Italian) parsley, leaves only, thinly sliced

Preheat the oven to 250°F.

TO MAKE THE DUCK CONFIT: Season the duck legs with salt and pepper and place, skin side up, in a 12 by 17-inch oven-safe dish. Sprinkle the garlic and thyme over the duck legs. Pour the duck fat over the legs. Don't worry if the legs aren't fully covered in the fat; they will render out more fat as they cook.

Cover the dish with foil and then place in the oven for anywhere between 2½ to three hours, until the leg meat is very tender. When cooked, removed the

pan from the oven. If you aren't using the duck legs immediately, let them cool and store them in the refrigerator. As long as the legs are fully submerged in fat, they should hold for up to three weeks. If you are using the duck legs right away, take the legs out of the pan and strain the fat into a clean container. Allow the fat to cool and set aside to be used later for sautéing.

Place a nonstick, 10-inch sauté pan on the stovetop over medium heat and add about two tablespoons of the reserved duck fat. When the fat has melted and is smoking hot, add the duck legs skin side down and let them cook, untouched, until the skin turns brown and crispy; this should take anywhere from one to two minutes. Once the skin is fully browned, turn the legs over and sear the meat side. If the skin sticks to the bottom of the pan when you try to turn the leg over, it's not done searing. You may need to cook the duck legs in batches to avoid overcrowding the pan. Once all of the duck has been seared, set aside until ready to use.

TO MAKE THE POTATOES: Add another three table-spoons of the duck fat to the same pan and then add the potatoes. Cook until the potatoes are browned on all sides. Once browned, add the shallots and garlic and cook until brown. Season with salt and pepper. Add the vinaigrette to the pan toss together with the potatoes to lightly coat.

TO SERVE: Dress the frisée with Le Marais Vinai-grette and divide the salad evenly among the plates. Place a crispy duck leg on top of the frisée and gar-nish each plate with potatoes and some parsley.

Soups

Chefs have a tendency to overthink things. We make our food out to be more important and significant than it really needs to be. Soup should be pure simplicity; the results are the sum of what you put into the pot – whether it's leftover bones from a roast chicken, beef bones from last night's prime ribs, or a mix of vegetables from the refrigerator that need to go somewhere other than the trash bin. Great soups are a reflection of your mood, your emotions, and of the current environment that you're in. The beauty of the soup pot is that it does most of the work for you; skills and rules for the most part need not apply.

Soup au Pistou

Serves 8 to 10

I *was brought up in a home with an Italian mother, and this soup was called a minestrone. Maybe not exactly the same soup, but pretty darn close.*

Pistou:

4 cups loosely packed fresh basil

½ cup extra virgin olive oil

1 teaspoon kosher salt

3 cloves garlic, peeled, roasted, and cooled

1 fresh plum tomato, rinsed and cored

Juice of 1 lemon

Salt and freshly ground black pepper

Soup:

¼ cup extra-virgin olive oil

2 ounces smoked veal bacon (optional), cut into lardons (see page 28)

5 cloves garlic, peeled and sliced

3 medium-sized carrots, peeled and cut into ¼-inch dice

2 ribs celery, cut into ¼-inch dice

1 small Spanish onion, peeled and cut into ¼-inch dice

1 medium-sized zucchini, cut into ¼-inch dice

¼ head savoy cabbage, cored and thinly sliced

1 (28-ounce) can whole peeled tomatoes

8 cups chicken stock (page 3)

½ cup small pasta, such as farfallini or elbows

1 (15-ounce) can cannellini beans, rinsed and drained

Kosher salt and freshly ground black pepper

TO MAKE THE PISTOU: Place all of the ingredients in the bowl of a food processor fitted with the blade attachment and purée until coarsely ground. Season to taste with salt and pepper. Set aside in the refrigerator until ready to use or for up to six hours.

TO MAKE THE SOUP: Place a 6-quart saucepan on the stovetop over medium-high heat and add the oil. Add the bacon and cook, stirring often, until it browns evenly and all of the fat has rendered out. Remove the bacon and drain on a clean paper towel until ready to use as part of the garnish.

Add the garlic, carrots, celery, and onion to the same pan as the rendered fat. Lower the temperature on the stovetop to medium heat and cook until the vegetables are tender yet crisp, about 10 to 12 minutes.

Add the zucchini and cabbage and cook until the cabbage has wilted, about three to five minutes. Add the tomatoes and the stock and bring to a boil. Season with salt and pepper and lower the temperature on the stovetop to low heat. Cook, simmering, for 20 minutes.

Place half of the beans in a bowl and use a fork to smash them into a paste. Mix this into the simmering soup. Then add the remaining beans and the pasta and cook for another eight minutes. Check the seasoning and serve, garnished with pistou and bacon.

This soup can made in advance, cooled and stored in the refrigerator, covered, for up to five days. Gently reheat the soup on the stovetop before serving.

ROASTED TOMATO AND EGGPLANT SOUP

SERVES 10

I was first taught this soup 20 years ago by chef Ralph Keutel at my first NYC restaurant called Stingray. It has become a favorite of mine to serve in the restaurant as well as a favorite at home with my wife, Sara. This is my, I'm in deep trouble and need a quick marriage fix soup. At home I like to garnish this with grilled baguette slices and crumbled goat cheese.

8 fresh plum tomatoes

6 cloves garlic, peeled

Salt and freshly ground black pepper

¼ cup extra virgin olive oil, plus extra for roasting

6 sprigs rosemary, divided

2 medium-sized eggplants

1 medium-sized Spanish onion, peeled and cut into ½-inch dice

½ medium-sized fennel, bulb only, cleaned and cut into ½-inch dice

Preheat the oven to 375°F. Place the tomatoes and garlic on a clean baking sheet and season them well with salt and pepper. Coat them liberally with oil. Place three of the rosemary sprigs on top of the vegetables and roast in the oven for about 25 minutes, or until the tomatoes are nicely browned in color and soft to the touch. Remove them from the oven, and hold at room temperature until they go into the soup.

Use a sharp knife to cut off the vine end, or stem, of the eggplants. Stand the eggplants upright, cut side down, and slice the eggplants in half lengthwise, or from north to south. Place them on a cutting board skin side down and use a sharp knife to score the flesh of the eggplant in an X pattern. Coat well with oil, and season with salt and pepper. Place the eggplant on a clean baking sheet, skin side down. Place the remaining rosemary springs on top of the eggplant and roast in the oven for about 30 minutes, or until the inside of the eggplant is soft enough to

be scooped out with a spoon. Let cool. Scoop out the flesh with a spoon and hold at room temperature while preparing the rest of the recipe. Discard the eggplant skins.

Place a 4-quart saucepan on the stovetop over medium heat and add the ¼ cup of oil. Add the onions and fennel and cook until soft, about eight minutes. Add the roasted tomatoes and garlic, as well as all of the juices from the pan. Add the eggplant and rosemary. Pour in 6 cups of water, bring to a simmer and cook, simmering, for about 40 minutes.

Working in batches, purée the soup in the container of an electric stand blender until smooth. You can also use a handheld immersion blender and purée the soup directly in the saucepan. Season to taste with salt and pepper and serve.

This soup can made in advance, cooled and stored in the refrigerator, covered, for up to five days. Gently reheat the soup on the stovetop before serving.

ROASTED JERUSALEM ARTICHOKE SOUP

SERVES 8

The sunchoke is one of those ingredients that have been fully embraced by chefs and not yet by the cooking public. To the naked eye, it looks kind of gnarly and unappealing. However, inside is a delicious dish just begging to be noticed.

2½ pounds Jerusalem artichokes (also called sunchokes), left whole

5 tablespoons extra virgin olive oil, divided

Salt and white pepper

8 ounces veal bacon, diced

1 leek, white part only, sliced

2 celery stalks, coarsely chopped

1 cup button mushrooms, sliced, stems intact

1 (750-ml) bottle dry white wine, such as moscato or sémillon

1 fresh bay leaf

1 bunch thyme

6 black peppercorns

4 quarts chicken stock (page 3), or vegetable stock or water

3 tablespoons freshly chopped flat leaf (Italian) parsley

Preheat the oven to 400°F.

Place the sunchokes in a colander and wash them thoroughly under cold water. Drain the sunchokes and place them on a clean baking sheet. Toss the sunchokes with 3 tablespoons of the oil, and season with salt and pepper. Bake in the oven until tender to the touch and slightly caramelized, about 25 to 30 minutes. The caramelization is an important step as it will add flavor to the soup.

Place a 4-quart stockpot on the stovetop over medium-high heat and add the remaining 2 tablespoons of oil. Add the bacon and cook until crisp and brown, rendering out the fat. Remove the bacon from the pan and drain on a paper towel until ready to use as part of the garnish.

Add the leeks, celery, and mushrooms to the same pot as the rendered fat and cook until soft but not browned. Stir in the wine and raise the temperature on the stovetop to high heat. Cook until the wine has reduced by three-quarters.

Place the thyme, peppercorns, and bay leaf in the center of a piece of cheesecloth and tie it up with butcher's twine to create a bag, or bundle. Toss the bag into the pot, add the roasted sunchokes, and add the stock. Bring everything to a boil and then lower the temperature on the stovetop to low heat. Let the soup cook, at a simmer, for about 45 minutes. While the soup cooks the stock will reduce down and all the flavors will develop. When ready, remove the herb bundle and season the soup with salt and pepper.

Working in batches, purée the soup in the container of an electric stand blender until smooth. You can also use a handheld immersion blender and purée the soup directly in the saucepan. Season to taste with salt and pepper. Garnish the soup with bacon and parsley and serve.

[SIDENOTE: If the soup is too thin, place it in a saucepan on the stovetop over medium heat and cook until reduced to a consistency of your liking. Likewise, if the soup is too thick, thin it out with additional stock or even water.]

This soup can made in advance, cooled and stored in the refrigerator, covered, for up to five days. Gently reheat the soup on the stovetop before serving.

ROASTED BUTTERNUT SQUASH SOUP WITH CAYENNE SEEDS

SERVES 8

2 large butternut squash

1 teaspoon ground cayenne pepper

3 tablespoons extra virgin olive oil, plus extra for cooking

1 small Spanish onion, peeled and cut into ¼-inch dice

2 ribs celery, cut into ¼-inch dice

1 small carrot, cut into ¼-inch dice

1 cinnamon stick

1 teaspoon ground cloves

6 leaves sage

4 cups chicken stock (page 3), or as needed

Kosher salt

Ground white pepper

Preheat the oven to 400°F.

Use a large knife to cut the squash in half lengthwise. Scoop out the seeds with a spoon. Rinse any pieces of squash from the seeds and toss the seeds in a bowl with the cayenne pepper. Spread the seeds single layer onto a clean baking sheet and roast in the oven until crisp, about 20 minutes. Remove the seeds from the oven and cool until ready to use. These can be made a week in advance and stored in an airtight container at room temperature.

Liberally coat the inside of the squash with oil and place cut side down in a 9 by 13-inch roasting pan. Add about ½ inch of water to the bottom of the pan. Place the squash in the oven and roast for about 45 minutes, until the water has evaporated and the squash has started to caramelize on the bottom.

Remove the squash from the oven and set aside to cool. When cool enough to handle, use a spoon to scoop out the meat and discard the skin.

Place a 4-quart saucepan on the stovetop over medium heat and add the oil. Add the onions, celery, and carrots and cook until soft and lightly caramelized. Tie the cinnamon stick, clove, and sage together in a cheesecloth bag and add it to the pot. Stir in the cooked squash and pour in enough chicken stock to cover the vegetables. Season with salt and white pepper and simmer for about 30 minutes.

Remove the spice bag. Working in batches, purée the soup in the container of an electric blender until smooth. You can also use a handheld immersion blender and purée the soup directly in the saucepan. When ready to serve, spoon the soup into individual bowls and garnish with a sprinkle of cayenne-baked squash seeds.

This soup can made in advance, cooled, and stored in the refrigerator, covered, for up to five days. Gently reheat the soup on the stovetop before serving.

Parsnip and Apple Soup

Serves 12

¼ cup extra virgin olive oil

1 medium-sized Spanish onion, peeled and cut into ¼-inch dice

2 cloves garlic, peeled and sliced

3 pounds medium-sized parsnips (about 8 pieces), peeled and cut crosswise into rounds

6 Granny Smith apples, peeled, cored and sliced

2 cups dry white wine, such as riesling

2 teaspoons ground coriander

8 cups chicken stock (page 3), or water

Salt and white pepper

Place a 6-quart saucepan on the stovetop over low heat and add the oil. Add the onions and garlic and cook gently until soft and translucent. Add the parsnips, apples, white wine, and coriander. Cook until the wine has reduced by half and then add the stock. Cook, simmering, until all of the vegetables are very tender, about 30 minutes.

Working in batches, purée the soup in the container of an electric stand blender until smooth. You can also use a handheld immersion blender and purée the soup directly in the saucepan. Season to taste with salt and pepper.

This soup can made in advance, cooled and stored in the refrigerator, covered, for up to five days. Gently reheat the soup on the stovetop before serving.

CHARRED CORN CHOWDER WITH BACON, CORN, AND LIME RELISH

SERVES 8

Chowder:

9 stalks corn, divided

Kosher salt and white pepper

6 tablespoons extra virgin
olive oil, divided

9 ounces smoked veal bacon, cut
into lardons (see page 28)

1 medium-sized Spanish onion,
peeled and cut into ¼-inch dice

2 ribs celery, cut into ¼-inch dice

2 cloves garlic, peeled and sliced

1 small bunch thyme, leaves
only, coarsely chopped

2 fresh bay leaves

½ teaspoon ground turmeric

3 cups chicken stock (page 3)

3 medium-sized Russet potatoes,
peeled and cut into ¼-inch dice

Relish:

Reserved bacon

3 stalks' worth reserved kernels

1 small bunch cilantro, freshly chopped

Zest of 2 small limes

Preheat the grill to high.

TO MAKE THE CHOWDER: Season the corn well with salt, pepper, and 3 tablespoons of the extra virgin olive oil. Place the corn on the hot grill and grill to a good, even char throughout. Remove the corn and set aside to cool. When cool enough to handle, carefully cut off the kernels and reserve, discarding the stalks. Measure out the kernels to be used as follows: 6 stalks' worth for the chowder, 3 stalks' worth for the relish.

Place a 4-quart saucepan on the stovetop over medium heat and add the oil and bacon. Cook the bacon until brown and crispy. Remove one-third of the bacon and drain on a clean paper towel until ready to use in the garnish.

Add the onion, celery, and garlic to the same pan as the remaining bacon and rendered fat, and sweat, or cook gently, until the vegetables are soft and cooked

all of the way through. Add the thyme, bay leaves, turmeric, and chicken stock and bring to a simmer. Season with salt and pepper. Add the reserved 6 stalks' worth of kernels to the pot along with the potatoes. Lower the temperature on the stovetop to low heat. Cook the soup at a simmer for about another 45 minutes.

Working in batches, purée the soup in the container of an electric blender until smooth. You can also use a handheld immersion blender and purée the soup directly in the saucepan. Season to taste with salt and pepper.

TO MAKE THE RELISH: Place the remaining 3 stalks' worth of kernels, the reserved bacon, the cilantro, and the lime zest in a bowl and toss to combine. Season with salt and pepper.

TO SERVE: Divide the soup evenly among bowls and top with 1 tablespoon of relish.

CUBAN BLACK BEAN SOUP

SERVES 8

3 tablespoons extra virgin olive oil

4 ounces smoked veal bacon, cut into ¼-inch dice

1 medium-sized Spanish onion, peeled and cut into ¼-inch dice

4 cloves garlic, peeled and sliced

1 red bell pepper, seeded, de-ribbed and cut into ¼-inch dice

1 (28-ounce) can black beans, drained

2 sprigs rosemary

Salt and freshly ground black pepper

⅓ cup apple cider vinegar

1 small fresh tomato, seeded and cut into ¼-inch dice

2 bunches scallions, coarsely chopped

6 sprigs cilantro

Place a 3-quart saucepan on the stovetop over medium heat and add the oil and bacon. Cook the bacon until brown and crisp. Remove the meat from the pan and drain on a paper towel-covered platter until ready to use at the end for garnish.

Add the onion, garlic, and red pepper to the same pan as the rendered fat and cook until softened. Stir in the beans and rosemary, and season with salt and pepper. Add enough water to the pan to cover everything by about two inches and bring everything to a boil. Lower the temperature on the stovetop to low heat and simmer for 45 minutes. Stir in the vinegar and cook for another 15 minutes.

Working in batches, purée the soup in the container of an electric stand blender until creamy and smooth. You can also use a handheld immersion blender and purée the soup directly in the saucepan. Serve the soup garnished with diced tomato, scallions, the reserved bacon, and some cilantro leaves.

This soup can made in advance, cooled and stored in the refrigerator, covered, for up to five days. Gently reheat the soup on the stovetop before serving.

FRENCH GREEN LENTIL SOUP

SERVES 10

While you can use your basic green lentil for this soup, I highly recommend making the effort to get the French green lentils that are specified below. They hold their form and texture much better than the standard lentils, which are starchier and break down. I also highly recommend getting a hunk of smoked veal bacon, it's a night-and-day difference from the beef fry that is on the market. Beef fry? Just sounds nasty. Call Dominique for the bacon.

3 tablespoons extra virgin olive oil

6 ounces smoked veal bacon, optional (not really – get it!), diced

1 large Spanish onion, peeled and cut into ¼-inch dice

3 ribs celery, cut into ¼-inch dice

1 medium-sized carrot, peeled and cut into ¼-inch dice

1 leek, white part only, cleaned and cut into ¼-inch dice

4 cloves garlic, peeled and sliced

1 tablespoons tomato paste

Salt and freshly ground black pepper

3 quarts chicken stock (page 3), or water

1 small bunch fresh thyme and 2 fresh bay leaves, tied together with kitchen string

1 (16-ounce) box French green lentils

Flat leaf (Italian) parsley, leaves only, for garnish

Place a 4-quart stockpot on the stovetop over medium heat and add the oil and bacon. Cook the bacon until brown and crisp. Remove the meat from the pan and drain on a paper towel-covered platter until ready to use at the end for garnish.

Add the onions, celery, carrots, leeks, and garlic to the same pan as the rendered fat and cook until just softened. Stir in the tomato paste and cook for another three minutes. Season the vegetable mixture with salt and pepper. Pour in the stock, add the herb bundle, and bring everything up to a boil. Add the lentils to the pot and lower the temperature on the stovetop to low heat. Bring the soup to a simmer, season with salt and pepper, and simmer for about 45 minutes. The lentils should be soft to the bite, yet still holding their shape and texture.

Garnish each bowl with some of the reserved bacon and parsley leaves and serve.

Kale, Italian Sausage, and Butter Bean Soup

Serves 10

For the record, Italian food isn't what you get at most American restaurants. I call that pizzeria cuisine. Random pastas and protein parmesans with pathetic canned sauces is not how Italy eats. This is a peasant's dish that is served as a meal along with the perfect loaf of semolina bread.

¼ cup extra virgin olive oil

½ pound Italian sausage (about 4 to 6 links), casings removed

1 medium-sized Spanish onion, peeled and cut into ¼-inch dice

4 cloves garlic, peeled and sliced

1 small carrot, peeled and cut into ¼-inch dice

2 quarts chicken stock (page 3)

1 (28-ounce) can whole tomatoes, drained and diced

2 bunches Tuscan kale, cleaned, stemmed, and thinly cut into 2-inch lengths

1 small bunch thyme

Salt and freshly ground black pepper

2 (19-ounce) cans butter beans, drained and rinsed

Place a heavy-bottomed, 4-quart stockpot on the stovetop over medium heat and add the oil. Add the sausage and cook, breaking up the meat until it browns slightly, about three minutes. Add the onion, garlic, and carrots and cook for another five minutes. Stir in the chicken stock, tomatoes, and the kale. Season with the salt and pepper and add the thyme.

Simmer the soup for about 30 minutes and then add the butter beans. Lower the temperature on the stovetop to low heat and let the soup simmer for another 30 minutes. Check the seasoning and serve.

This soup can made in advance, cooled, and stored in the refrigerator, covered, for up to two days. Gently reheat the soup on the stovetop before serving.

ITALIAN WEDDING SOUP

SERVES 8

General meatball-making rule: meatballs are panfried, not roasted in the oven. Period. Take the extra few minutes – as always, the extra few minutes make all of the difference.

Meatballs:

4 tablespoons extra virgin olive oil, divided

1 small Spanish onion, peeled and cut into ¼-inch dice

4 teaspoons sliced garlic

Salt and freshly ground black pepper

2½ pounds ground veal

1½ cups white bread, crusts removed, cut into ¼-inch dice

6 tablespoons flat leaf (Italian) parsley, freshly chopped

3 large eggs, beaten

Soup:

1 large white onion, peeled and cut into ¼-inch dice

4 medium-sized carrots, peeled and cut into half moons

4 ribs celery, cut into ¼-inch dice

3 quarts chicken stock (page 3)

2 cups dry white wine, such as chardonnay

2 cups small pasta, such as elbows or tubetini

½ cup minced dill

2 packages washed baby spinach

Salt and freshly ground black pepper

TO MAKE THE MEATBALLS: Place an 8-inch skillet on the stovetop over medium heat and add 2 tablespoons of the oil. Add the onion and garlic and cook until softened and caramelized. Season with salt and pepper. Remove the pan from the stovetop and set the mixture aside to cool.

Place the cooled onion mixture in a large bowl with the veal, bread, parsley, and eggs and mix well by hand to combine. By hand, or with a small ice cream scoop, form the mixture into 1-inch-round meatballs.

Place a 10-inch saucepan on the stovetop over high heat and add the remaining 2 tablespoons oil. When the pan is hot, add the meatballs and brown very well on all sides. You may need to cook the meatballs in batches to avoid overcrowding the pan. Drain the meatballs on a paper towel-covered platter and set aside until ready to use. The meatballs can be made up to two days in advance and stored in the refrigerator until ready to use.

TO MAKE THE SOUP: Add the onions, carrots, and celery to the same saucepan as the rendered fat and cook until the vegetables caramelize and are cooked all of the way through. Stir in the chicken stock and wine and bring everything to a boil. Add the pasta, lower the temperature on the stovetop to low heat, and let the soup simmer for another four minutes. Add the meatballs and dill. Stir in the spinach two minutes before serving, giving the spinach just enough time to start to wilt but still have some texture.

Taste the soup, season with salt and pepper and serve with a side of semolina bread.

CHICKEN POSOLE SOUP

SERVES 10

This has become one of my more popular soup options. I always need to make extra because the staff goes ape over it. Posole is also known as hominy. Hominy is a food made from kernels of corn that are soaked in an alkali solution of either lime or lye. The corrosive nature of the solution removes the hull and germ of the corn and causes the grain itself to puff up to about twice its normal size. More often than not, white corn is used instead of yellow. Make this, and the Latinos in your life will stave off their planned coup for at least a day or so. Works for me.

4 teaspoons extra virgin olive oil

6 ribs celery, cut into ¼-inch dice

2 medium-sized carrots, peeled and cut into ¼-inch dice

2 medium-sized Spanish onions, peeled and cut into ¼-inch dice

½ large fennel, bulb only, cleaned and cut into ¼-inch dice

3 cloves garlic, peeled and sliced

1 teaspoon fennel seeds

2 tablespoons chili powder

½ teaspoon cumin seed

½ cup instant or all-purpose flour

2 tablespoons tomato paste

1 (3½-pound) whole chicken

Salt and white pepper

1 bunch rosemary

1 fresh bay leaf

1 small bunch cilantro, plus extra for serving

1 (28-ounce) can posole

Place a 4-quart stockpot on the stovetop over medium heat and add the oil. When hot, add the celery, carrots, onions, garlic, and fennel and cook until tender and lightly browned. Stir occasionally to prevent the vegetables from burning on the bottom of the pan. Add the fennel seeds, chili powder, and cumin seed and cook gently for an additional five minutes.

Sprinkle the flour over the vegetables and stir well with a wooden spoon until combined. The flour will cause the mixture to thicken quickly and begin to stick to the bottom of the pan. That's OK. Let it cook for about three minutes, being careful not to let it scorch. Stir in the tomato paste and cook an

additional three minutes. Add the chicken to the pot and add enough water to cover the chicken. Season the soup with salt and pepper, and add the rosemary and bay leaf. Bring everything to a boil, then lower the temperature on the stovetop to low heat and let everything simmer for one hour, or until the chicken is cooked all of the way through.

Once the chicken is cooked all of the way through, remove it from the pot and set aside to cool.

Add the posole to the same stockpot and cook, at a simmer, for another 45 minutes.

When the chicken is cool enough to touch, remove

the meat from the bones, discarding the skin and bones. Add the chicken meat to the pot. Skim the fat from the top of the simmering soup as necessary, and season the soup with salt and pepper.

Serve garnished with whole cilantro leaves. The addition of cooked white rice makes for a delicious stew and a hearty meal.

This soup can made in advance, cooled, and stored in the refrigerator, covered, for up to three days. Gently reheat the soup on the stovetop before serving.

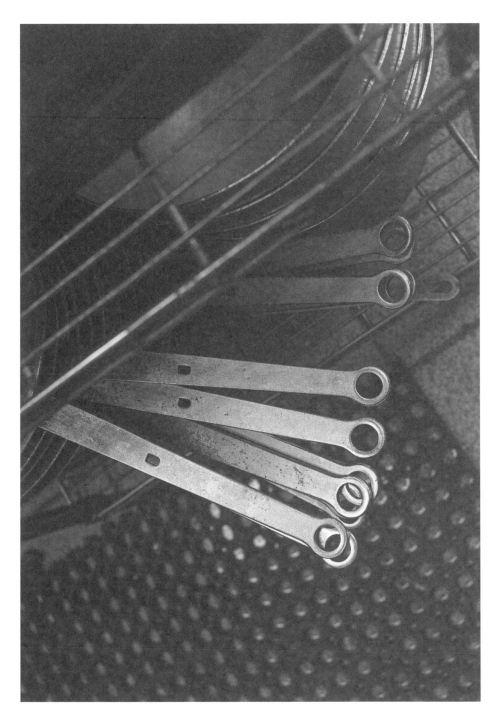

Appetizers

I have some very vivid memories of my childhood. For me, the most vivid are not of the happy/carefree variety. The ones that have stuck in my head are the most awkward, uncomfortable, and unpleasant moments. Somehow, these are the moments that make me smile more than the seemingly benign, joyful times.

To this day, when I eat out with my family I can still hear my mother's voice rattling around my brain. "You don't need appetizers, they're too expensive. Who needs that much food anyway, it's not good for you!" Uugghh.

Fast-forward to today: meals at my house are always a ridiculous multicourse meal and I *always* order appetizers for my kids when we go out. I suggest you do as well.

ASSIETTE DE CRUDITÉS

SERVES 6

*W*ith the exception of an obnoxiously drunk relative talking politics, nothing is worse at a party than the plate of sad-looking vegetables with a pathetic dip to accompany it. Does anybody eat this? This isn't what crudités should be, as the French know full well. Consider it more as a dish of small salads that someone actually put some thought into. The varieties are endless; these are just a few ideas.

The cold dishes can and should be made as much as three hours in advance. Remove them from the refrigerator a ½ hour before you serve them to bring them up to room temperature.

Time the cooking of the hot food so that you can serve it fresh from the oven.

Cucumber Salad:

½ seedless English cucumber, thinly sliced crosswise

1 small shallot, peeled and thinly sliced

Juice of 1 lemon

4 sprigs tarragon, leaves only, coarsely chopped

2 tablespoons extra virgin olive oil

Salt and white pepper

Place the cucumber, shallot, lemon juice, and tarragon in a small bowl and mix to combine. Drizzle with oil and season with salt and pepper.

Shredded-Carrot Salad:

2 small carrots, peeled and coarsely shredded

1 small bunch flat leaf (Italian) parsley, leaves only, coarsely chopped

½ cup dried currants, soaked in ½ cup hot water and drained

Juice of 1 lemon

Small drizzle of honey

Extra virgin olive oil

Salt and freshly ground black pepper

Place the carrots, parsley, drained currants, lemon juice, and honey in a small bowl and mix to combine. Drizzle with oil and season with salt and pepper.

Cherry-Tomato Salad:

1 pint cherry tomatoes,
rinsed and stemmed

Zest and juice of 3 limes

6 leaves basil, thinly sliced

Extra virgin olive oil

Salt and freshly
ground pepper

Place the tomatoes, lime zest, lime juice, and basil in a small bowl and mix to combine. Drizzle with oil and season with salt and pepper.

Roasted Sugar Snap Peas:

2 cups sugar snap peas, cleaned

2 tablespoons extra virgin
olive oil

1 medium-sized shallot,
peeled and minced

4 sprigs thyme, leaves only

Coarse sea salt

Preheat the oven to 400°F.

Place the peas, oil, shallots, and thyme together in a bowl and toss to combine. Spread the mixture evenly out onto a baking sheet and roast in the oven for six minutes. While still hot from the oven, sprinkle with the salt.

EGGS MAYONNAISE

SERVES 8

In food and fashion there is always one constant: what's old is now new again. The eggs mayonnaise is an old-school French bistro dish that is desperately trying to make a comeback and may very well do so since the restaurant industry is now getting tired of tweezer food. So join me in putting on my parachute pants and mesh shirts and let's make some eggs.

Mayonnaise (page 18)
8 extra-large eggs, hard-boiled and peeled (see note)

8 slices toasted baguette
Flat leaf (Italian) parsley, thinly sliced, for garnish

When ready to serve, slice the eggs in half and place one half on top of each slice of baguette. Coat with some mayonnaise and sprinkle with parsley. Serve with a small, crisp salad dressed with a simple vinaigrette.

[SIDENOTE: Everyone boils eggs, and everyone overcooks eggs. But boiling an egg properly isn't as cut and dried as you may think. Here is a foolproof method: Place your eggs in a pot large enough to hold them comfortably, and then cover them with cold water. Place that pot onto the stovetop and bring it up to a boil. Once the eggs reach a boil, take the pot off of the fire. Let the eggs sit in the hot water off of the fire for exactly 12 minutes. After 12 minutes, remove the eggs from the hot water and immediately place them in a bowl of ice water to shock the eggs and stop the cooking. Cooling the eggs down quickly and in this manner will also make them significantly easier to peel. If you do as I ask, your yolks will be creamy instead of dry as death with that nasty green ring around the outside. The whites will be soft and tender, instead of like a white rubber band.

Tuna Tartare with Mango, Avocado Purée, and Cilantro

Serves 8

For plating, use a tall round mold. A piece of PVC pipe or a tall 2-inch ring mold will do the job nicely. I always torture my fishmonger and tell him to cut out the blood line and the nervy piece. If I'm already paying over $20 a pound, I expect that it all be useable.

A few tips on buying tuna. First, the tuna loin should be displayed whole and then cut to order. Cut steaks will begin to oxidize, and turn brown quickly. Also, look for gapping. Gapping is when the meat of the muscle starts to separate and flake. The filet should be from a ruby red to pink color with a shiny, slick look to it. Like all fresh fish, it should smell sweet like the ocean, not fishy.

Tuna tartare:

1 (1½-pound) sushi-grade Yellowfin tuna loin, trimmed (see note)

2 small shallots, peeled and finely diced

Zest of 2 limes

1½ tablespoons extra virgin olive oil

2 tablespoons freshly chopped cilantro

Sea salt and white pepper

Tabasco, to taste

Avocado purée:

2 ripe avocados, pitted and peeled

Juice of 2 limes

1 tablespoon extra virgin olive oil

Salt and white pepper

Garnish:

2 ripe Champagne mangos

Salt and white pepper

Micro-cilantro or cilantro leaves

Herb oil (optional)

Mango purée (optional)

TO MAKE THE TUNA: Cut the clean tuna into a ¼-inch dice and place the cubes in a non-reactive bowl. Cover the bowl with plastic wrap and chill in the refrigerator for up to four hours before serving.

[SIDENOTE: It's important to remove the blood line from the tuna loin, as it is bitter and inedible. While I recommend asking your fishmonger to do this for you, if you decide to try it on your own, use the tip of a sharp knife and be careful to only remove the blood line. Next, flip over the tuna and locate the area on the bottom of the loin that is striped with white nerves. Gently slice that off as well, as the nerves are tough and chewy and will ruin the texture of the tartare.]

TO MAKE THE AVOCADO PURÉE: Place the avocado meat in the bowl of a food processor fitted with the blade attachment. Add the lime juice and oil, season with salt and pepper, and purée until very smooth.

Peel the mango and remove the meat from the pit. Use a sharp knife to cut the mango meat into a small dice. Season with salt and pepper.

Remove the tuna from the refrigerator. Add the shallots, lime zest, oil, cilantro, Tabasco, salt and pepper to the bowl and gently toss all the ingredients together.

TO SERVE: Place the mold in the center of a plate and fill about one-third full with tuna. Next add a layer of mango and then a layer of the avocado purée to finish. Gently lift off the mold, there should be little or no resistance. Repeat with remaining plates. Garnish the top of each tower with cilantro leaves.

OPTIONAL: Drizzle with herb oil and store-bought mango purée.

STEAK TARTARE

SERVES 6

The French bistro, in essence, is what it is because of this dish. Take that sneering look off your face, and just try it. The creamy, rich texture is just irreplaceable. Good toasted baguettes on the side are a necessity. Just like every other food that you eat raw, fresh beef is a must. One more thing: give me a break with being afraid of a raw egg yolk. It isn't 1920! The CDC says that only 1 in 20,000 eggs have salmonella. I'll take those odds.

2 large egg yolks

2 tablespoons Dijon mustard

2 teaspoons ketchup

2 drops Tabasco sauce

Salt and freshly ground
black pepper

¼ cup peanut oil

1 tablespoon cognac

1 small white onion, peeled
and finely chopped

¼ cup capers, drained and rinsed

¼ cup cornichons, drained
and finely chopped

4 sprigs flat leaf (Italian)
parsley, finely chopped

1¼ pounds freshly ground lean rib eye

Place six plates in the refrigerator to chill.

Place the yolks and mustard in a stainless steel bowl and whisk to combine. Add the ketchup, and Tabasco, season with salt and pepper, and mix well. Slowly whisk in the oil, then add the cognac and whisk again. Fold in the onions, capers, cornichons, and parsley.

Add the ground beef to the bowl and use a spoon or rubber spatula to mix well. Taste and check for seasoning.

Divide the tartare evenly among the chilled plates and serve with crusty bread or toasted croutons.

MARINATED WHOLE GRILLED SARDINES WITH FENNEL SALAD AND FINE HERB SAUCE

SERVES 8

It's not easy to come across fresh sardines, but if you have the opportunity, take advantage of it. You can substitute any other fatty fish for the sardines and it will work just fine. Tuna, escolar, and local blue fish will all work well.

Fine herb sauce:

½ cup freshly minced chives

½ cup loosely packed, fresh flat leaf (Italian) parsley, coarsely chopped

⅓ cup extra virgin olive oil

½ small red onion, peeled and minced

Juice of 1 lemon

Salt and white pepper

Fennel salad:

1 medium-sized fennel, bulb only, cleaned and shaved on a mandolin or thinly cut into 2-inch lengths

Juice of 2 lemons

Salt and white pepper

Extra virgin olive oil

Sardines:

16 fresh sardines, heads and tails intact

3 cloves garlic, peeled and sliced

2 tablespoons coarsely chopped flat leaf (Italian) parsley

2 teaspoons extra virgin olive oil

Sea salt

8 slices toasted baguette, for serving

TO MAKE THE HERB SAUCE: Place the all of the ingredients in a bowl and mix to combine. Refrigerate the sauce until ready to serve. Allow the sauce to come to room temperature before using.

TO MAKE THE FENNEL SALAD: Place the all of the ingredients in a bowl and mix to combine. Cover with plastic wrap and refrigerate until ready to serve.

TO MAKE THE SARDINES: Lay the sardines side by side in a non-reactive, 3-quart baking dish. Sprinkle the fish with garlic and parsley, drizzle with oil, and season with copious amounts of sea salt. Cover the

dish with plastic wrap and refrigerate for at least one hour or up to two.

Preheat the grill until it's nice and hot. Be patient, if the grill isn't hot enough the sardines will stick to the grates. When ready, grill the sardines for three to four minutes per side, or until the skin is charred and crisp.

To serve, spoon some herb sauce onto each slice of baguette, place a sardine over the sauce, and top with some of the fennel salad.

RED MULLET ESCABECHE

SERVES 8

Dishes such as this are the norm in all of the coastal communities in Spain and Portugal. Which, of course, is why this recipe is here – the boss is Portuguese and my ass is on the line. The most vital part of any fish dish is that the fish is impeccably fresh. Get to know your fishmonger, flirt if you must, to get the freshest product available and a heads up on when he gets the good stuff.

8 whole red mullet, scaled, filleted, pin bones removed

Salt and freshly ground black pepper

½ cup extra virgin olive oil

Escabeche marinade:

2 cups extra virgin olive oil

1 medium-sized red onion, peeled and thinly sliced

2 cloves garlic, peeled and sliced

1 cup malt vinegar

½ cup good quality green olives, pitted and sliced

Salt and freshly ground black pepper

Garnish:

1 small bunch flat leaf (Italian) parsley, coarsely chopped

TO COOK THE FISH: Season the fillets with salt and pepper. Place a 10-inch skillet on the stovetop over medium heat and add the olive oil. When the oil begins to slightly smoke, add the fillets to the skillet skin side down, and brown them on this side only. Transfer the fillets to a paper towel to drain. Once drained, lay the fillets side by side in a non-reactive, 9 by 13-inch shallow baking dish.

TO MAKE THE MARINADE: Place a 2-quart saucepan on the stovetop over medium heat and add the oil. It may seem like way too much oil, but trust me that it works. When the oil is hot, add the red onion and garlic. Cook for about two minutes, just until

they are soft and translucent. Add the vinegar and olives, and season with salt and pepper. Remove the pan from the heat and cool slightly, about four minutes.

While the marinade is still warm, pour it over the fish. Cover the dish with plastic wrap and refrigerate overnight. Cover the dish while it is still warm, so that the residual steam helps cook the fish.

The next day, remove the fish from the refrigerator and bring to room temperature before serving. Garnish the fish with parsley and serve over crisp greens that have been dressed with the marinade in place of vinaigrette.

SALMON CAKES

MAKES 8 CAKES

Without question, the most popular of all fish that we serve at the restaurant is salmon. We receive salmon deliveries at the restaurant five days a week. But then I have to figure out what to do with all the scraps from the salmon butchering. For this recipe I'll also throw in some of the scraps from the smoked-salmon butchering.

1½ pounds fresh salmon, skinned and cut into ¼-inch dice	6 sprigs cilantro, coarsely chopped
1 small red onion, peeled and cut into ¼-inch dice	⅓ cup Dijon mustard
2 ribs celery, cut into ¼-inch dice	⅔ cup fresh mayonnaise (page 18)
1 cup cornichons, minced	3 drops Tabasco sauce
¼ cup capers, minced	Salt and white pepper
6 sprigs parsley, coarsely chopped	3 cups Japanese-style dry bread crumbs
	½ cup extra virgin olive oil

Place the salmon, onion, celery, cornichons, capers, parsley, cilantro, mustard, mayonnaise, and Tabasco in a large bowl and mix to combine. Season with salt and pepper. By hand, form the mixture into eight 3-ounce cakes, about 2½ inches in diameter by ¾-inch thick each.

[SIDENOTE: Don't make the cakes any thicker than one inch or they may not cook all of the way through.]

Place the bread crumbs in a large bowl. Dip the salmon cakes on all sides until thoroughly coated with bread crumbs. Place the salmon cakes on a clean plate and chill in the refrigerator for at least one hour before pan-frying.

Place a nonstick, 10-inch frying pan on the stovetop over medium heat and add the oil. You are not sautéing here; this is a pan fry and therefore calls for lots of oil. When the oil begins to shimmer and slightly smoke, add the salmon cakes one by one, leaving space in between so that they cook evenly and brown properly. You may need to cook the salmon cakes in several batches to avoid overcrowding the pan. Once the cakes are nicely browned, carefully flip them over and brown the other side. The salmon cakes should take no more than three to four minutes per side; this should allow them to crisp up and cook all of the way through. When ready, remove them from the pan and drain on a paper towel-covered plate.

Serve immediately with a green salad or with red cabbage slaw (page 216).

PAN-ROASTED BREAST OF DUCK WITH FRENCH GREEN LENTIL SALAD

SERVES 8

A duck breast is always an elegant component to a meal. The elements of this can all be made in advance and then just put together at the service time. The cardinal sin is to overcook the breast; the highest acceptable temperature is medium, and even that is pushing it. If it doesn't have a pink hue throughout the entire breast, it's overcooked.

Lentils:

3 tablespoons extra virgin olive oil

1 medium-sized carrot, peeled and cut into ¼-inch dice

1 medium-sized red onion, peeled and cut into ¼-inch dice

1 small fennel, bulb only, cleaned and cut into ¼-inch dice

1½ cups dry French green lentils, rinsed and drained

1 small bunch thyme

1 fresh bay leaf

Salt and white pepper

Duck:

4 fresh whole duck breasts

Salt and freshly ground black pepper

Vinaigrette:

3 tablespoons red wine vinegar

1 teaspoon Dijon mustard

1 small shallot, peeled and minced

½ cup extra virgin olive oil

Salt and white pepper

Garnish:

3 sprigs flat leaf (Italian) parsley, leaves only

TO MAKE THE LENTILS: Place a 10-inch skillet on the stovetop over medium heat and add the oil. Add the carrot, red onion, and fennel and cook slowly, without color, until they become somewhat translucent; this should take no more than four to five minutes. Add the lentils to the pan and mix them in with the vegetables. Add enough cold water to the pan to cover the lentils by at least one inch. Add the thyme and bay leaf, and season with salt and white pepper. Raise the temperature on the stovetop to high heat and bring everything to a boil. Lower the temperature on the stovetop to low heat and bring to a simmer. Cook, simmering, for about 20 minutes. Taste the lentils for doneness: you will know the lentils are properly cooked when they are soft all of the way through, yet still firm enough to hold their shape.

[SIDENOTE: If the lentils need to cook longer add more water in 1-cup intervals, allowing the water to be fully absorbed each time. The lentils must maintain their integrity, meaning that they must still have a firm texture and not become mushy.]

When ready, spread the lentils out in a single layer onto a clean baking sheet to cool. Remove and discard the herbs. Refrigerate until the lentils are cold to the touch.

TO COOK THE DUCK BREAST: Use a sharp chef's knife to score an x pattern into the fat on the back of each breast (see page 141). Place a 10-inch skillet on the stovetop over low to medium heat. Add the breasts, fat side down, and let cook, untouched; it will take about eight to 12 minutes for the breasts to brown and for all of the fat to render off. Leave the breasts be, do not futz with them during this process. Once you see that about three tablespoons or so of fat has rendered into the pan, use a pair of tongs to gently lift the breasts and take a look. If most of the white fat has rendered out and the remaining skin is crispy and brown, the duck breasts are ready to be flipped. Flip over each breast and sear them meat side down for another three minutes. Remove the breasts from the pan and place them on a cutting board fat side up. While the duck is hot, season both the fat and the skin side with salt and black pepper. Allow the duck breasts to rest on the cutting board for 10 minutes before slicing into them. Pour the rendered duck fat into a container and store for later use; it can be used as a wonderful fat for roasting potatoes.

TO MAKE THE VINAIGRETTE: Place the vinegar, mustard, and shallots in a small bowl and whisk until combined. Slowly drizzle in the oil while whisking continuously until all of the oil has been added and the dressing has emulsified. Season with salt and pepper.

TO SERVE: Place the lentils in a bowl and dress with the vinaigrette to your liking. Toss in the parsley leaves and season as necessary.

Use a sharp chef's knife to cut each of the duck breasts width-wise into even, ¾-inch-wide slices.

Divide the lentils evenly onto the centers of eight plates. Artfully layer about six slices of duck breast over each pile of lentils. Drizzle each plate with some of the remaining the vinaigrette.

Sautéed Veal Sweetbreads with Mango, Quinoa, Mache, and Star Anise Vinaigrette

Serves 6

Sweetbreads have always been considered a throwaway part of the veal, and thus inexpensive. Why else would they be categorized under a name as ugly as offal? Not anymore folks, these suckers have become so expensive on the kosher market that they are no longer a peasant's meal; they are now served on the most booshie of dining tables.

Sweetbreads:

2 pounds veal sweetbreads

1 bunch thyme

2 cloves garlic, peeled

1 lemon, halved

Salt and white pepper

Instant flour, for dredging

¼ cup extra virgin olive oil

Quinoa:

3 tablespoons extra virgin olive oil

1 small shallot, peeled and minced

1 rib celery, finely diced

½ small carrot, peeled and cut into ¼-inch dice

1 cup quinoa, rinsed and drained

2 cups chicken stock (page 3), or water

Salt and freshly ground black pepper

4 sprigs tarragon

Vinaigrette:

½ cup rice wine vinegar

1 teaspoon ground star anise

1 clove garlic, peeled and minced

1 tablespoon freshly squeezed lime juice

2 tablespoons freshly squeezed lemon juice

1 tablespoon turbinado sugar

½ cup peanut oil

Salt and freshly ground black pepper

To serve:

1 ripe mango, peeled and cut into ¼-inch dice

1 cup loosely packed mache

2 sprigs tarragon, leaves only

TO MAKE THE SWEETBREADS: Place a 3-quart saucepan on the stovetop over medium heat and add the sweetbreads, thyme, garlic, and lemon. Add in enough cold water to cover the sweetbreads, and bring the mixture to a boil. Lower the temperature on the stovetop to low heat, cover the pan, and simmer for about 1½ hours, or until the sweetbreads are cooked all the way through and very tender. Remove the sweetbreads from the pot and plunge them into a bowl of ice water to stop the cooking. Leave the sweetbreads in the ice water until the center of the meat has cooled, about 10 minutes.

Use your hands to remove the outer membrane from the cooled sweetbreads. To do this, peel away

what looks like the skin covering meat. Remove as much as you can to keep the finished product from being too chewy.

Cut the sweetbreads into bite-sized pieces and place them on a plate. Cover the plate with plastic wrap and store in the refrigerator until ready to use. Up to this point, the sweetbreads can be made up to three days in advance.

TO MAKE THE QUINOA: Place a 10-inch sauté pan on the stovetop over medium heat and add the oil. When hot, add the shallots, celery, and carrot and cook gently until all of the vegetables are soft and just slightly browned. Add the quinoa and toast in the hot pan for two minutes. Add the chicken stock, season with salt and pepper and toss in the tarragon. Bring the mixture up to a boil, then lower the temperature on the stovetop to low heat. Cook the quinoa at a simmer until all of the liquid is fully absorbed. Remove the pan from the stovetop, fluff the quinoa with a fork, cover the pan, and set aside while you finish preparing the dish.

TO FINISH THE SWEETBREADS: Place the flour in a bowl. Season the sweetbreads with salt and pepper. Toss the chilled sweetbread in the flour to completely coat, knocking off any excess.

Place a 10-inch skillet on the stovetop over medium heat and add the oil. . When the oil begins to shimmer and slightly smoke, add the sweetbreads and brown on all sides until very crisp. You may need to do cook them in batches to avoid over crowding the pan. Repeat until all of the pieces have been browned. Drain on a paper towel-covered plate.

TO MAKE THE VINAIGRETTE: Place the vinegar, star anise, garlic, lime juice, lemon juice, and sugar into the container of an electric blender. Cover and blend until completely smooth. While the blender is running, slowly add the peanut oil and season with salt and pepper.

TO SERVE: Mix the mango in with the quinoa and then lightly dress with vinaigrette.

Place the mache in a large bowl and dress with vinaigrette.

Divide the quinoa between six plates, or place all in the center of one large serving platter. Top the quinoa with sweetbread pieces, then with mache. Garnish with tarragon leaves and an extra drizzle of extra virgin olive oil. Your family should be thoroughly impressed. Hopefully impressed enough to leave at an appropriate hour.

VEAL SWEETBREADS WITH FOREST MUSHROOMS

SERVES 8

No, it's not brains!! I'll never forget a guest demanding my presence tableside and then arrogantly asking me to tell them what sweetbreads were. When I said veal thymus glands, he defiantly insisted upon just how wrong I was and then proceeded to tell his dinner guests just how little this "chef" actually knows. Not that it bothered me or anything.

Finding wild mushrooms isn't always the easiest thing to do. If you have a local farmers' market, this would be your best resource. If that isn't available to you, move. If moving isn't in the cards, then use a combination of shitakes, creminis, and oyster mushrooms. All of these are cultivated and widely available in supermarkets.

Sweetbreads:

3 pounds veal sweetbreads

1 bunch thyme

3 cloves garlic, peeled

2 lemons, halved

Salt and white pepper

Instant flour, for dredging

¼ cup extra virgin olive oil

Mushrooms:

4 tablespoons extra virgin olive oil

1 medium-sized shallot, peeled and sliced

3 cloves garlic, peeled and sliced

1½ pounds wild forest mushrooms

5 sprigs thyme

1 pint veal stock (page 2)

To serve:

8 large slices toasted baguette, cut on the bias

Flat leaf (Italian) parsley, freshly chopped, for garnish

TO MAKE THE SWEETBREADS: Place a 3-quart saucepan on the stovetop over medium heat and add the sweetbreads, thyme, garlic and lemon. Add in enough cold water to cover the sweetbreads and bring the mixture to a boil. Lower the temperature on the stovetop to low heat, cover the pan and simmer for about 1½ hours, or until the sweetbreads are cooked all the way through and very tender. Remove the sweetbreads from the pot and plunge them into a bowl of ice water to stop the cooking. Leave the sweetbreads in the ice water until the center of the meat has cooled, about 10 minutes.

Use your hands to remove the outer membrane from the cooled sweetbreads. To do this, peel away what looks like the skin covering meat. Remove as much as you can to keep the finished product from being too chewy.

Cut the sweetbreads into bite-sized pieces and place them on a plate. Cover the plate with plastic wrap and store in the refrigerator until ready to use. Up to this point, the sweetbreads can be made up to three days in advance.

TO MAKE THE MUSHROOMS: Place a 10-inch sauté pan on the stovetop over medium heat and add the oil. Add the shallots and garlic and cook until lightly caramelized, about four minutes. At the same time, place the mushrooms in a bowl and cover with cold water. Use your hands to agitate the mushrooms to release the dirt. Drain off the water as soon as possible: you do not want the mushrooms to absorb any of the water. Add the mushrooms and the thyme to the hot pan. Allow the mushrooms to cook until almost all of the water has been released and has evaporated from the pan, about 10 minutes. Raise the temperature on the stovetop to high heat and add the veal stock to the pan. Cook until reduced and thickened. Lower the temperature on the

stovetop as much as possible, so that it is just hot enough to keep the sauce warm while you finish the sweetbreads.

TO FINISH THE SWEETBREADS: Place the flour in a bowl. Season the sweetbreads with salt and pepper. Toss the chilled sweetbread in the flour to completely coat, knocking off any excess.

Place a 10-inch skillet on the stovetop over medium heat and add the oil. When the oil begins to shimmer and slightly smoke, add the sweetbreads and brown on all sides until very crisp. You may need to cook them in batches to avoid overcrowding the pan. Repeat until all of the pieces have been browned. Drain on a paper towel-covered plate.

TO SERVE: Place one baguette slice in the center of each plate. Top with pieces of sweetbread and cover with wild mushroom sauce. Garnish with parsley.

Lamb Chili with Avocado Mousse

Chili:

3 tablespoons extra virgin olive oil

1 medium-sized Spanish onion, peeled and cut into ¼-inch dice

3 cloves garlic, peeled

2 ribs celery, cut into ¼-inch dice

1 large red bell pepper, de-ribbed, seeded, and cut into ¼-inch dice

1 teaspoon cumin seeds

1 teaspoon fennel seeds

1 teaspoon red pepper flakes

2 teaspoon chili powder

1½ pounds ground lamb

Salt and white pepper

3 tablespoons tomato paste

1 (28-ounce) can whole peeled tomatoes, drained and crushed by hand

1 (10-ounce) can garbanzo beans, rinsed and drained

4 sprigs rosemary

4 sprigs mint

Avocado mousse:

2 ripe avocados, pitted and peeled

Juice of 2 small limes

1 small bunch cilantro, leaves only

Salt and white pepper

TO MAKE THE CHILI: Place a 6-quart saucepot on the stovetop over medium heat and add the oil. When the oil begins to lightly smoke, add the onion, garlic, celery, and bell pepper and cook gently until the vegetables are soft and translucent.

Add the cumin, fennel, pepper flakes, and chili powder and stir to combine. Cook for about four minutes to allow the spices to properly toast and release their flavor.

Raise the temperature on the stovetop to high heat and add the ground lamb, breaking the meat apart as it cooks. Cook for about five minutes, or until the meat is slightly browned. Season with salt and pepper. Stir in the tomato paste and cook for another five minutes. The tomato paste will begin to brown and thicken the meat mixture. Add the tomatoes

and garbanzo beans, along with one tomato can full of water, and stir well to combine. Tie the mint and the rosemary together with a piece of kitchen twine and add that to the pot. Reduce the temperature on the stovetop to low heat and let the chili simmer for at least two hours. During this time, skim off any excess fat from the surface of the chili and discard.

TO MAKE THE AVOCADO MOUSSE: Place all of the ingredients in the bowl of a food processor fitted with the blade attachment and purée until smooth and very creamy. Remove the mousse from the food processor and store in a plastic or glass bowl.

[SIDENOTE: An aluminum bowl may react with the acid from the lime and discolor the mousse and impart a metallic flavor.]

If you are not serving it right away, cover the mousse

with plastic wrap. The wrap needs to be placed direct-ly on top of the mousse, not just the bowl, in order to prevent oxidation on the surface of the mousse.

When ready to serve the chili, taste and adjust the seasoning; it may need some additional rosemary or mint. Garnish the chili with avocado mousse.

SLOW-COOKED SHORT RIBS WITH SPICY MUSTARD SAUCE

SERVES 8

This is when buying that backyard smoker finally makes sense. Incredibly easy to prepare with amazing results.

Ribs:

2 medium-sized Spanish onions, peeled and cut into ½-inch dice

3 ribs celery, left whole

1 large carrot, peeled and cut into 1-inch pieces

5 cloves garlic, peeled

5 pounds beef short ribs

Salt and freshly ground black pepper

Mustard sauce:

1 cup Dijon mustard

½ cup rice wine vinegar

½ cup apple cider vinegar

¼ cup molasses

½ teaspoon ground cayenne pepper

Salt

Preheat the oven to 195°F.

TO MAKE THE RIBS: Place the onions, celery, carrots, and garlic in a 17 by 12 by 3-inch lidded roasting pan, and add two cups of water to the bottom of the pan.

Season the short ribs generously with salt and pepper. Lay the meat on top of the vegetables and then place the pan into the oven. Cook slowly for 17 hours, cooking covered for the first 10 hours and then uncovered for the last seven. The ribs are ready when they are soft and tender when pinched, and you are able to pull the meat apart easily with your hands.

TO MAKE THE SAUCE: Place all of the ingredients in a bowl and whisk together to combine. The beauty of this sauce is that this can be made well in advance and then stored in the refrigerator without any negative reaction. It can be stored in the refrigerator for up to one month, as long as the temperature remains stable.

Serve the ribs as is and let your guests gnaw at the bones, or remove the bones and neatly portion the meat into 2½-inch cubes.

BEEF RIBS

When I was first presented with this product my initial response was to say, "Are you kidding me? Are we so devoid of variety that you are now giving me this garbage?" So I decided to smoke and slow cook them. Go figure, they were amazing! If you have a smoker, some light smoke definitely adds to it, but you can live without it.

10 to 12 beef ribs (about 8 pounds)

Salt and coarsely ground black pepper

2 medium-sized Spanish onions, peeled and coarsely chopped

1 large carrot, peeled and cut crosswise into ½-inch-thick slices

3 ribs celery, coarsely cut into 1-inch pieces

4 cloves garlic, peeled and coarsely chopped

Preheat the oven to 195°F.

Season the beef ribs liberally with salt and pepper. Place the onions, carrot, celery, and garlic in a 17 by 12 by 3-inch roasting pan. Place the ribs on top of the vegetables. Pour two cups of water into the bottom of the pan; this will prevent the vegetables from burning while also adding moisture to the ribs. Cover the roasting pan with aluminum foil, leaving one corner open to allow steam to escape.

Place the ribs in the oven and slow roast for 10 hours. At this point the ribs should be a rich, brown color and the meat should be tender, but not falling off of the bone.

Bread & Pasta

Has there been any food product in the last 25 years that has gotten as bad a rap as has the noble grain of wheat? That wheat and its protein, gluten, have taken such a beating is beyond belief in my book (and this is my book!). Celiac disease is a true problem that about 1 in 100 people deal with. For the rest of us, wheat products – just like everything else – should be eaten in moderation.

That being said, I could cut anything from my diet without too much issue, with the exception of pasta and bread. I could easily live on it, and would gladly die for it. I love you, wheat, always have, always will.

RUSTIC CORNBREAD

MAKES ONE 8 BY 8-INCH CORNBREAD

I think that we have all had our share of pathetic cornbread. Its dry, falls apart, and of all of the things that it may taste like, corn sure as hell isn't one of them. Problem solved. It may take a little extra effort, but worth every second. Use frozen corn here even when fresh is available. The frozen corn will actually be sweeter because they are frozen soon after being picked.

1 pound (4 sticks / 2 cups) unsalted margarine, room temperature, plus extra for greasing the pan

1 cup plus 2 tablespoons cake flour, plus extra for dusting

2 (16-ounce) bags frozen corn kernels

1 cup plus 1 tablespoon whipped topping

2 large eggs, beaten

¾ cups finely ground cornmeal

1 cup granulated sugar

1 tablespoon salt

1 teaspoon baking powder

½ teaspoon baking soda

4 tablespoons freshly chopped thyme, leaves only

Preheat the oven to 350°F. Grease an 8 by 8-inch baking pan with margarine and dust with flour, making sure to shake out any excess.

Place an 8-inch skillet on the stovetop over high heat. Add the margarine and corn and sauté until the corn is well browned. Be a little patient, this could take longer than you may think, anywhere between 12 to 15 minutes. Place the cooked corn in the container of an electric blender. Add the whipped topping and the eggs, cover the container with its lid, and purée the mixture until very smooth.

Place the flour, cornmeal, sugar, salt, baking powder, baking soda, and thyme in a bowl and mix to combine. Use a spatula to fold in the puréed corn mixture until incorporated. Transfer the mix to the prepared pan.

Pay attention to this part as this is where you have the potential to screw this up. Place the pan in the oven and bake for 10 minutes. Then lower the oven temperature to 265°F and bake for an additional 25 minutes, or until a toothpick inserted into the center of the bread comes out dry.

Remove the pan from the oven. Let the cornbread cool to room temperature before removing it from the pan and slicing. The cornbread will keep in an airtight container or well wrapped in plastic wrap for three to four days, at room temperature.

LE MARAIS COOKBOOK · 91

ROSEMARY FOCACCIA

MAKES 2 LOAVES

When making the sour starter, or sponge, I recommend that you make a double batch. The starter can be stored indefinitely and the flavor only improves with age. Indefinitely means indefinitely. Good, old-school bread bakers will keep their starters for years. Mine at the restaurant is over 2 years old as of the writing of this. When I eventually get fired, I will be taking my knives and my sour with me.

Sour starter:
1/16 teaspoon active dry yeast
½ cup cold water
½ cup plus 3 tablespoons bread flour

Focaccia dough:
1¼ cups water, body
temperature 98°F to 100°F

½ cup extra virgin olive oil,
divided, plus extra for coating
1 recipe sour starter
1¾ teaspoons active dry yeast
3⅔ cups bread flour, plus extra as needed
1½ tablespoons kosher salt
4 tablespoons freshly chopped rosemary

TO MAKE THE STARTER: You will need to make the starter at least two days before making the bread. Place the yeast, water and flour in a bowl and whisk to combine. Store at room temperature in a tightly sealed container for a minimum of two days. More is best. Like I said earlier, chefs keep this stuff around for years. When you remove the needed amount of starter, replace it with the same volume of equal parts of water and bread flour. For example, if you remove 2 cups of starter, whisk back in 1 cup of water and 1 cup of bread flour. Then seal it up until the next time you use it. Just remember to give it a quick mix before using.

TO MAKE THE BREAD DOUGH: Place the water, 1 tablespoon of olive oil and the sour starter in the bowl of a stand mixer fitted with a dough hook. With the mixer on low speed, add the yeast and the

flour and mix until a dough forms. With the mixer running, add the salt and the rosemary. Increase the mixer speed to medium and mix the dough for another six minutes. After six minutes, the dough should pull away from the inside of the bowl. If it doesn't, sprinkle a little more flour into the bowl and continue to mix until it does.

Lightly oil a bowl large enough to hold the dough when it doubles in size with olive oil. Place the dough in the bottom of the oiled bowl and cover the bowl tightly with plastic wrap. Set aside at room temperature until the dough doubles in size; depending on the warmth of the room, this could take between 1½ to two hours.

When the dough is ready, remove it from the bowl and place it onto a clean, lightly floured work surface. Gently fold the edges of the dough in toward

the center. Flip the dough over and repeat, folding the edges toward the center to form a ball. Place the dough back into the oiled bowl, cover tightly with plastic wrap and let it proof for at least one additional hour.

Add ¼ cup of the oil to each of two round 10-inch diameter cake pans. Tilt the pans from side to side, until the oil coats the entire bottom of each pan.

Gently turn the proofed dough out onto a clean, lightly floured work surface, being careful not to deflate the dough. Use a knife to divide the dough into two equal pieces. Place one piece into each of the prepared pans. Cover each pan with a clean cloth and set aside at room temperature for about 30 min-

utes, to allow the dough to relax and proof until it spreads across the bottom of each pan.

While the dough is proofing in the pans, preheat the oven to 425°F and center a rack in the middle of the oven. When the dough is fully proofed, place the pans in the oven and bake for 15 minutes. Rotate the pans 180 degrees, and bake for an additional 15 minutes. Remove the pans from the oven and immediately unmold the loaves onto a baking rack to cool.

Once baked, the focaccia will hold at room temperature for about two days. After that, the bread can be sliced and used as toast or diced and baked for croutons.

POTATO GNOCCHI WITH ITALIAN SAUSAGE AND BROCCOLI RABE

SERVES 8

Gnocchi is a form of pasta that, if made properly, is light and airy, yet always satiates a hunger. It's homey quality makes it an all-time favorite of mine. When you add the richness and fattiness of an Italian sausage and the bitterness from the rabe, you get an awesome meal. I personally always add some heat to my broccoli rabe, but that's up to you. (Do it.)

The most important part of the gnocchi-making procedure is the cooking of the potato. Removing all of the moisture from the potato is the key to keeping the gnocchi light and airy instead of heavy and gummy. Also, don't overwork the dough. If it gets overworked, the dough will get over starched, and therefore gummy.

Gnocchi:

3 large Idaho potatoes, scrubbed

2 tablespoons extra virgin olive oil

Kosher salt

1 to 1¼ cups all-purpose flour

1 large egg

To serve:

Extra virgin olive oil

1½ pounds cooked sweet or spicy

Italian sausage, cut crosswise into ½-inch-thick rounds

4 fresh plum tomatoes, seeded and diced

Pinch red pepper flakes

1 bunch broccoli rabe, blanched and shocked (see page 220), cut into small pieces

8 sprigs fresh oregano

Salt and white pepper

Zest of 1 lemon

TO MAKE THE GNOCCHI: Preheat the oven to 400°F. Dust a baking sheet with flour and set aside.

Bake the potatoes in the oven until tender, about one hour. If the tip of a small knife is easily inserted into the center, the potatoes are done. Set aside to cool slightly.

Peel the cooled potatoes, and then press them through a ricer or through a fine mesh strainer onto a lightly flowered surface. Drizzle the oil over the potatoes and add a small pinch of salt. Slowly sprinkle the flour over the potatoes, mixing by hand just until the flour is well incorporated. Make a well in the middle

of the mixture. Crack the egg into the well. Use your fingertips to gather the potato-flour mixture into the egg a little at a time, adding more flour if the dough is very sticky. When the dough forms a smooth but slightly sticky ball, knead in another small pinch of salt. Cut the dough into four equal pieces.

Clean the work surface and lightly dust it with flour. Working with one piece of dough at a time, roll it out under your palms to form a long smooth rope, about ½ inch thick. Cut each rope into ¾-inch-long pieces and place them on the prepared baking sheet. Repeat until all of the dough has been rolled and cut.

Place a 4-quart stockpot on the stovetop over high heat, fill with water and bring to a boil. Working in batches of 20 pieces at a time, drop the gnocchi into the boiling water. Once the gnocchi start to float, they are ready. Remove the cooked gnocchi from the pot and submerge them in a bowl of ice water for about 60 seconds to stop the cooking. Remove the gnocchi from the ice water and set them aside onto an oiled sheet tray until ready to use. At this stage they can be chilled and stored, covered, for up to two days in the refrigerator.

TO FINISH THE DISH: Place a 10-inch sauté pan on the stovetop over medium heat and add the oil.

When hot, add the gnocchi. You want the gnocchi to take on some color, so let them brown.

[SIDENOTE: When sautéing the gnocchi, it is essential to start with a very hot pan, otherwise the gnocchi will stick.]

Once the gnocchi are nicely browned, add the sausage, tomato, and pepper flakes and let cook for about one minute. Add the wine, broccoli rabe, and oregano and toss to combine. Season with salt and white pepper and add the lemon zest.

Divide the gnocchi evenly among the plates and drizzle with extra virgin olive oil just before serving.

Crazy Good Biscuits

Just flat-out sick. 'Nuff said. This recipe is worth the cost of the book on its own. Assuming that you paid for it.

Biscuits:

3¾ cups all-purpose self-rising flour, plus extra for dusting

2 tablespoons granulated sugar

1 tablespoon baking powder

2 teaspoons salt

12 tablespoons (1½ sticks / ¾ cup) unsalted margarine, frozen

2 cups whipped topping, very cold

Egg wash:

1 large egg

2 tablespoons water

TO MAKE THE BISCUITS: Preheat the oven to 350°F. Line a baking sheet with parchment paper and set aside.

Place the flour, sugar, baking powder, and salt in a bowl and mix together by hand to combine. Use a box grater to grate the margarine over the bowl of dry ingredients. Gently mix in the margarine by hand. The goal here is to gently coat all of the margarine with the flour mixture.

[SIDENOTE: Grating the margarine is the most important part of the recipe as this allows for nearly perfect fat distribution throughout the biscuits.]

Slowly drizzle in the whipped topping, incorporating by hand until the mixture just begins to form into a dough; it should still be a little bit sticky. Lightly flour the dough and form it into a ball. Let the dough rest in the refrigerator for at least one hour before using.

Place the chilled dough onto the prepared baking sheet and then gently pat the dough into a ½-inch-thick rectangle. Use either a floured chef's knife or a dough cutter to cut the dough into 16 square biscuits. Separate the biscuits on the baking sheet, leaving enough space in between to allow for them to spread.

[SIDENOTE: I cut the dough into squares so that there isn't any waste. You could certainly cut the biscuits into circles if you wish. If you do cut them into circles, gather up the scraps, reform the dough into a disk and refrigerate for at least another hour before you use it.]

TO MAKE THE EGG WASH: Place the egg and water in a small bowl and whisk to combine. Use a pastry brush to brush the tops of the biscuits with the egg wash.

Place the biscuits in the oven and bake until the tops turn golden brown. This should take about 15 to 17 minutes.

RAGÙ BOLOGNESE

SERVES 6

This is now your go-to meat sauce. Make a big batch, break it down into smaller containers, and freeze it. Drop the frozen sauce directly into a saucepan, get it hot, boil pasta – instant meal.

¼ cup extra virgin olive oil

1 medium-sized Spanish onion, peeled and cut into ¼-inch dice

2 celery stalks, cut into ¼-inch dice

1 medium-sized carrot, peeled and cut into ¼-inch dice

5 cloves garlic, peeled and sliced

1 teaspoon red pepper flakes

2 teaspoons fennel seeds

1 pound ground veal

1 pound ground beef

2 tablespoons tomato paste

½ (750-ml) bottle dry red wine, such as a merlot, pinot noir, or whatever you have

1 (28-ounce) can whole plum tomatoes, crushed by hand, juice reserved

6 sprigs thyme

6 sprigs basil

Salt and freshly ground black pepper

½ cup flat leaf (Italian) parsley, freshly chopped

Place a 4-quart saucepot on the stovetop over medium heat and add the oil, onions, celery, carrots, and garlic. Sauté the vegetables until soft and translucent, with no color, about eight minutes. Add the red pepper flakes and fennel seed and sauté for about a minute, to allow the flavor of the spice to develop. Add the ground meat and cook, stirring frequently, until the meat is browned and the fat has rendered out. This should take about 10 to 12 minutes.

Stir in the tomato paste and cook for another two minutes. Add the wine, tomatoes, thyme, and basil. Season with salt and pepper. Lower the temperature to a simmer and cook on very low for three hours, until thickened. The longer you cook the sauce, the deeper the flavors will develop.

When ready to use, toss with a hearty shaped pasta, such as rigatoni or pappardelle, and garnish with parsley before serving.

SUNDAY DINNER OF FUSILLI LUNGHI, MEATBALLS, AND BRACIOLE

SERVES 8

Every culture has its own version of a Sunday dinner. It is the one mandatory time of the week when everyone drops what they're doing and sits down to feast. When I was a kid, not attending led to a series of whacks to the back of the head as well as so much guilt that it continues to manifest itself inside the depths of my soul to this very day. Besides, who in their right minds would miss what is the holy grail of meals.

Mom would always preach that there are Italians and then everyone else who wished that they were. I'm not sure how true this is, but come Sunday at 2:00 p.m. I sure as hell felt that way. Sunday dinner is always between two and three o'clock, not quite sure why. It doesn't matter – if you make this just right, you'll just know that that's the way it should be.

Preparation must begin by 7:00 a.m. This is vital. Waking up from a deep sleep to the smell of frying meatballs is such a glorious experience that I pity those who never had the visceral pleasure. So start early and make them drool all day in anticipation. Besides, the meat needs to slowly braise the day away. This is where the sauce gets its monster flavor.

Meatballs:

¼ cup extra virgin olive oil

4 cloves garlic, peeled and thinly sliced

1 medium-sized yellow onion, peeled and cut into ¼-inch dice

1 pound ground beef

1 pound ground veal

2 large eggs, beaten

2 cups soft white bread, crusts removed, cut into ¼-inch dice

2 cups fresh basil leaves

Salt and freshly ground black pepper

Braciole:

4 (4-ounce) pieces veal, thinly pounded

Salt and freshly ground black pepper

2 cups fresh or good quality, store-bought bread crumbs

1 large egg

8 sprigs flat leaf (Italian) parsley, leaves only, coarsely chopped

Sauce:

¼ cup extra virgin olive oil

Italian Sausage, optional but recommended. Available from the Le Marais butcher's window.

1 medium-sized yellow onion, peeled and cut into ¼-inch dice

4 cloves garlic, peeled and thinly sliced

3 (28-ounce) cans whole plum tomatoes

Salt and freshly ground pepper

1 bunch basil

Pasta:

Kosher salt

2 pounds pasta: fusilli lunghi, bucatini, spaghetti, or your favorite pasta

TO MAKE THE MEATBALLS: Place an 8-inch sauté pan on the stovetop over medium heat. Add the oil, garlic, and onions and cook until golden brown. Remove the pan from the stovetop and cool the mixture to room temperature.

Place the onion mixture, beef, veal, eggs, bread, basil, salt and pepper in a bowl and mix thoroughly by hand. Form the mixture into whatever size meatball that you desire. Place them on a plate in the refrigerator while you work on your braciole.

[SIDENOTE: Allowing the meatballs to fully cool and rest in the refrigerator before cooking makes them easier to work with.]

TO MAKE THE BRACIOLE: Season each piece of veal with salt and pepper and lay flat on a clean work surface. Place the breadcrumbs, egg, and parsley in a bowl and mix to combine. Divide the filling evenly among the veal pieces. Roll up each piece of veal and tie each in three places to hold them together during frying and braising.

TO MAKE THE SAUCE: Place an 8-quart stockpot on the stovetop over medium-high heat and add the oil. When the oil is hot, add the meatballs, braciole, and Italian sausage and brown thoroughly on each side, to form a deep, richly colored crust. Remove the browned meat from the pot and set aside on a paper towel-covered platter to drain and until ready to place into the sauce.

[SIDENOTE: Use a pot that is wide and shallow versus deep and narrow for best results when browning the meat.]

Carefully remove about one-quarter of the hot cooking oil from the pot and discard. To the remaining oil add the onions and garlic, and lower the temperature on the stovetop to medium heat. Add the reserved liquid from the canned tomatoes to the pot. Crush the canned tomatoes in your hands and add those to the pot as well. Let the sauce come up to a simmer. Season with salt and pepper.

Return the meat to the pot and lower the temperature on the stovetop to a very low heat. The sauce should not boil or even simmer. It should be hot with only the occasional bubble popping up through the surface.

Add the basil and let the sauce cook very, very gently for about 3½ hours. The longer the sauce cooks, the more it reduces and the flavor intensifies. Gently stir occasionally to be sure that you are not burning the bottom, keeping an eye on the cooking temperature. Taste the sauce after the first three hours and see if the depth of flavor is to your liking. This is a very personal decision. I like to let it cook for four hours, but you make the call for yourself.

When the sauce is done, get the pasta working. The general rule for cooking pasta is 1 gallon of water per pound of pasta. Salt the pasta water very liberally.

[SIDENOTE: I get that "liberally" is a subjective term, so let me put it like this. A chef at the CIA, who will remain anonymous, told me the following: "When salting water for either pasta or blanching green vegetables, it should taste like the dead f'ing sea!" He may have been tactless, but he was dead on.]

Cook the pasta according to the manufacturer's directions. I can't give you any sense of cooking time as I don't know what kind of pasta you are using. Call me and tell me what you're using and I'll give you a number. The best advice that I can give you here is to cook the pasta to al dente, meaning it should not be soft and mushy. Properly cooked pasta should have a distinctive bite without any raw flavor. Give the pasta a stir every minute or so to keep it from sticking together as it cooks. Adding olive oil to the cooking water does not keep the pasta from sticking; it just makes the water taste good before you dump it down the drain. When the pasta is cooked, drain off the water.

To serve, put the hot pasta back into the cooking pot and add as much of the sauce as you like. Mix the pasta and the sauce so that all of the noodles are fully coated with the sauce. Serving a plain bowl of pasta and spooning sauce over it only works well for the Olive Gardens' photo shoots. Whatever you do, don't mimic the Olive Garden, ever.

THE LE MARAIS FRIES

At Le Marais, we take great pride in the product that we put onto the table. Countless hours and dollars are spent every year to ensure that the best possible product is put on your table and that we do it at a reasonable cost to our guests. I'm not taking you for a ride! Maybe a little. If you actually knew what went on behind closed doors all in the name of you, you would either be incredibly flattered or come to the conclusion that Jose and I are a couple of mental cases. Either way, simply perfect food isn't always that simple. Case in point, the French fry.

The French fry isn't actually a French creation, it's Belgian. I can only hope that this causes some Frenchmen somewhere great stress and pain. Without question, our fries are among the best in New York, kosher or not. Getting great fries isn't a secret. What it takes, however, is a great dedication of time and resources. Both of which really aren't in the cards for most home cooks.

Just like every other item on the plate, you start with the best ingredients. For a fry, the best potato is the Russet Burbank potato, also known as the Idaho potato. To be even more specific, we use the GPOD. GPOD is not a grower or a region, it's a coalition of growers who size, grade, and ship Idaho potatoes. For us, their real importance is the consistency of quality that we have never seen in any other brand of potatoes. This makes for a more expensive potato and better fries. If you decide to venture into the fry-making business at home, good luck going to the supermarket and getting GPODS. Not gonna happen. We buy 750 pounds a day, so we get whatever we want.

The next problem for the home cook is dealing with the oil. Anyone who has fried anything at home knows that the biggest problem is at the end of the cooking. How do I get rid of this mess? If you rent, you could pour it down the drain – it's not yours, right? You could dump it into the neighbor's bushes and then loudly proclaim in your best phony wonderment, "Hey, what happened to your hydrangea? Must be the other neighbor's dog." I guess the best answer would be to let it cool and then pour it back into the container from which it came. Assuming that the container is empty. At the restaurant, we have large barrels that we dump the oil into and then a recycling company comes and takes it away.

When deep frying you need lots of oil; without it the fries won't cook evenly. The best oil for the job is peanut oil. Peanut oil is the best because it has a neutral flavor as well as a high smoking point. The high smoking point lets us fry without concern that the oil will break down and get nasty. As always, the best comes with the price tag of the best. Pure peanut oil is the most expensive fry oil on the market and we use 175 pounds of it each day. We change the oil, without question, every day, regardless of the expense.

Perfection in French-fry cooking is also a timely process. All of those potatoes must be peeled, cut, blanched, cooled, and then fried again before they hit the plate. We have 2 people on the payroll with the sole purpose of making French fries. And a third guy who spends half of his day on it. That's a lot of labor cost to spend solely on one menu item. The things we do for you, and nobody appreciates it! This is why we can't have nice things! The point that I am trying to make here, if you haven't gotten there yet, is that you certainly can recreate our fries at home but there is no shortcut to it. So if you're in, then let's do this.

6 Russet Burbank, or Idaho Potatoes
Peanut oil for frying
Kosher salt

Peel the potatoes and place them in a bowl of ice water to keep the potatoes from oxidizing and turning brown. You can do this anywhere from 15 minutes to one day in advance. Trim the ends of the potatoes to square them off, and then cut them into ½-inch-thick sticks. Hold them in the water until you are ready to fry them. Easy, right? No so much.

If using a deep fryer, fill it about three-quarters full with oil and preheat to 300°F.

If not using a deep fryer, place an 8-quart stockpot on the stovetop over medium heat and fill it about half full with oil. Insert a candy thermometer and heat the oil until it reaches 300°F.

Line a baking sheet with paper towel or clean cloth and set aside.

Working in batches, blanch the potatoes in the hot oil for about six to nine minutes per batch. The potatoes should be cooked all of the way through but the outside should still be a pale white color. Remove the fries from the oil and spread them out evenly onto the prepared baking sheet to drain and cool.

Once all of the fries have been blanched, raise the temperature of the oil to 375°F. Still working in batches, refry the potatoes for two to three minutes per batch, or until they have reached the desired color and texture. The fries should be golden brown, crispy on the outside and light and fluffy on the inside. Remove the fries from the oil, allowing any excess to drain off, and place them in a large bowl lined with a cloth towel. Season the fries with salt while they are still hot and serve them immediately.

*L*ike I said earlier, the perfect fry is a process. Seems to me that it's much easier to make your way into Times Square to see us than it is to do it yourself. Try it once and you'll have a newfound appreciation for that golden brown pile of papas on your plate.

Beef

First things first: despite the claims of every pathetic beef-producing country in the world, American beef, without question, is the best damn animal, period. Quite frankly, the beef from places such as Argentina, Uruguay, Australia, and France all suck. I will take it one step further: equally awful are most kinds of hippie beef – grass-fed, humanely raised, coats daily brushed and conditioned with avocado extracts. There is a reason why wealthy countries pay out the snout to get their paws on USDA graded beef. The reason is grains. American cattle are finished with grain feeding instead of the all-grass feeding that the rest of the fools around the world use. The finishing grains are what gives the beef the extra fat and marbling (just like me!) that is necessary for a juicy and flavorful steak. So wave your flag, Americans, we may have lower math and science scores than the rest of the developed world, but no one tops our burgers!!!

So, where do you begin? The supermarket has lots of different cuts of meat sitting in Styrofoam trays all ready to go. Easy enough. But how do you know what to buy? Which cuts work best with the type of cooking that you are doing? Am I paying too much or for something that I am not actually getting? This is why when buying food, old school is always the way to go. Get to know your butcher, become friendly with him; he will best be able to steer you through the maze of yummy flesh.

At Le Marais, we have made it a point to have a French butcher, Dominique. They aren't always the most personable chaps, but they do know their way around a carcass. The French don't cut meat the way American butchers do. They are trained differently. A French butcher is taught how to use the entire animal, head to tail, with no waste. They have a tremendous respect for the animal that has so graciously given its life so that we can continue ours. This type of attitude is just now beginning to enter the American lexicon of artisanal butchery. Unfortunately, the vast majority of American butchers have never even put a knife to a whole animal. They are only familiar with the subprimal cuts for which you need very little imagination to turn into a steak or ground beef. As an example, if you give American butchers a shoulder cut, most will coarsely break it down into basic cuts for braising. The French will take the same cut, separate out the individual muscles from the shoulder into tender steaks for grilling, cubes for stewing, fillets for steak frites, you get the picture. The bottom line is that the French cut more; they therefore have more to offer their customers and are more cost effective for the restaurant.

Buying kosher beef is also a somewhat more complicated procedure than for your non-Jewish counterparts. The simple reason being that no kosher beef, I repeat, no kosher beef is graded by the USDA. It is all inspected by the USDA, but not graded. So if your butcher or restaurant tells you otherwise, he is either misinformed or just flat-out lying. The USDA does not require grading, so the kosher meat packers have decided against it. Don't believe me? Is your butcher is telling you otherwise? Ask your butcher to show you a piece of meat with the grading stamp on it. That's the way that it's done. A sticker on the side of the box placed there from the packer does not make it a prime piece of beef. Besides, the reality of the beef industry is that only about 2 to 4 percent of all beef that is graded by the USDA comes in at a prime grade. There just simply isn't enough prime quality beef on the market to be on all of those menus! My apologies to the rest of the industry, but someone had to say it. Since I'm not the most popular girl at the dance anyway, I don't feel bad about it. So what do you look for? Start with marbling. Marbling is

the veins of thin fat that runs through the muscle. The more marbling, the higher the grade. If very little to no marbling is seen in the muscle, this is graded as select quality. Select beef will yield a less tender piece of steak and a drier braised item. If the muscle has a good veining of white fat throughout, it will get the choice grading. This will yield a much more tender steak on the grill as well as a juicier beef bourguignon. To get the coveted prime grade, the muscle of the meat must have full integration of fat marbling throughout the entire muscle. A true prime steak is what our ideal of a grilled steak should be. Tender and juicy throughout. So use your eyes when buying a steak, that big bright red steak underneath that skin of plastic wrap just may not be for you. Ask your butcher to show you a whole, well-marbled rib and have him cut it to your specifications. Leave the trashy cuts in the plastic for the next guy.

We all have that member of the family, and it may be you, who will ask the waiter every time they go out to eat, "Is it fresh?" Have you ever gotten the answer, "So glad you asked that, because it smells like the Hudson at low tide"? Of course not. Yet when guests comes to us and asks that very same question about our beef, they are told, "Hell, no! Our meat is never fresh!" Eating fresh beef is like eating a loaf of bread without letting the yeast do its thing. Fresh beef is chewy as a rubber band and tastes just

as good. All of the beef at Le Marais goes through an aging process, and this makes it much more appealing. So what is aging? Aging is the process during which microbes and enzymes act upon the meat to help break down the connective tissue, for the sake of making the meat object more tender. Whether it happens in a bag (wet aging) or out in the air (dry aging), that element of the process is the same. For wet aging the meat is refrigerated in a plastic bag for at least 28 days. The plastic doesn't allow the meat to breathe, so it ages in contact with its own blood, which lends it a more intense, sour note and a more natural and bloody type of flavor. Dry aging, on the other hand, allows the meat to breathe, lose water (which increases its "beefiness," since there is now less water for the same amount of muscle fiber), and get acted upon by other microbes in the air besides just those of the muscle itself. Those other microbes are the long, threadlike mycelia of various airborne fungi that begin to digest the meat, giving an aged rib its distinctive flavor, aroma, and firm fleshed exterior. So which one is better? Depends upon who you ask and the cut you are aging. In order to dry age, the cut needs to have a thick layer of protective fat around it. Without this layer of fat, you would lose way too much of the meat itself to the trimming of that ultra-nasty looking exterior. This is why we only dry age a whole bone in rib eye. The rest of the meat we wet age. To some, the musky flavors from the rib

eye are a turn off. Others, especially food snobs and know-it-alls like myself, prefer the aged rib steaks.

Cooking temperatures are a whole different conversation. When having a well-marbled, aged steak, cooking it to anything above a medium rare is a sin and I believe that it should be a crime to do so. Just what would that poor steer think if he could have lived to see the disaster that is that over-charred lump of carbon on your plate? I do have somewhat of an understanding as to why many cultures overcook their beef. I believe that it's from years of the inundation of poor-quality meat that has been the mainstay of backyard grills as well as the kosher restaurants of the past. The beef was brutal, no marbleization, and so fresh that it was still flinching before it hit the grill. Well done was the only way that your body could muster up the necessary enzymes possible to digest that abomination. Thanks to Jose, kosher beef will never be the same and you can now safely order a proper steak. When cooking at home, how do you know when to remove a steak from the grill or the pan? Get yourself a digital meat thermometer and insert it into the thickest part of the meat. Use this temperature, along with the guide below, to help you in your grilling journeys.

Rare: The internal temperature will be between 120 and 125 degrees. When cut open, the middle will still be red with a dark pinkish hue throughout. It will be slightly warm to the touch.

Medium rare: The internal temperature will be between 130 and 135 degrees. When cut open, the center will be very pink and have some graying around the outer rim of the steak. The center will be warm to the touch.

Medium: The internal temperature will be between 140 and 145 degrees. When cut open, the center will be a mild pink color and the interior will be hot to the touch.

Medium well (oy!): The internal temperature will be between 150 and 155 degrees. When the steak is cut open, the steak will be mostly a grayish brown throughout with still a hint of pinkness.

Well done (oy gevalt!!): The internal temperature will be between 160 and 165 degrees. When the steak is cut open a puff of dust will come out. Actually, the meat will be uniformly grey and browned throughout and firm to the touch.

What cut do I need for my meal? Are you grilling, sautéing, braising, stewing? In America, we also seem to equate the tenderness of a cut of meat to the flavor. Not only not true, but generally the tough gnarly cuts of meat that require some work are without question the best-tasting pieces of the animal. Here are some of the most popular cuts at Le Marais, and the best ways to use them.

The rib eye steak: Without a doubt, the undisputed king of steaks. This cut has the perfect ratio of lean to fat to marbling. As well as just the best mix of flavor and texture on a steak. Needs to be either grilled or sautéed in a screaming hot pan.

The côte de boeuf: The bone in big-brother version of the rib eye. Same part of the animal except that we dry age this bad boy and it has the extra bonus of a bone that should be gnawed on until it's clean. Same cooking methods as the rib eye above.

The tournedo and the pepper steak: If you ask me, these are girly cuts. They are the eye only of the rib eye. The butcher cleans and removes all of the best parts, leaving you with a lean fillet. Searing in a hot pan and finishing in an oven is best.

The Le Marais surprise: This is the by-product of the above girly cuts. The surprise is the piece that is removed from the rib eye in order to create the tournedos. Because of this, we have a limited supply of surprise on most nights. My recommendation to you would be to encourage all of your friends to come in for a tournedo, thus leaving these well-marbled masterpieces all for you and everyone else who knows better. Sear either on a hot grill or sauté pan.

The onglet (the hanger steak): A quagmire of a kosher steak. Tremendous flavor, maybe the best in terms of pure flavor. However, also the saltiest after it is kashered. Best when cooked on a hot grill.

The Le Marais steak frites: We cut the steak frites from a cut called the silvertip. The silvertip is found in the shoulder. It makes for very good steak frites because of its wonderful flavor and its pleasantly chewy texture. The silvertip also allows for us to cut it into fairly thin slices, as is customary with steak frites. The best method of cooking is quickly, on a hot grill, not above medium rare.

The paleron: Also known as the chicken steak, this cut is absolutely perfect for your braising and stews. When of good quality, it is lined with marbling as well as intense gelatin for your sauce. If you catch Dominique on a good day, he may use some of those fresh butchery skills and cut you some nice flat iron steaks for the grill.

Short ribs: Also known to some as flanken, these have a strong beefy taste, are usually very well marbled, and have good sticky gelatin content as well. Perfect for braising and stews, and amazing for slow BBQ cooking.

Beef cheeks: This is the beast of all braising cuts. When slow cooked, the meat easily pulls apart and all of the sticky natural gelatin makes for an unforgettable sauce. This is a special order, so plan ahead.

Cabernet Braised Short Ribs of Beef

Serves 6

2 tablespoons peanut oil

6 individual beef short ribs

Salt and freshly ground black pepper

1 medium-sized Spanish onion, peeled and cut into ¼-inch dice

1 rib celery, cut into ¼-inch dice

1 small carrot, peeled and cut into ¼-inch dice

4 cloves garlic, peeled

2 tablespoons tomato paste

1 cup all-purpose flour

1 (750-ml) bottle cabernet sauvignon

1 bunch thyme

2 fresh bay leaves

Place a 6-quart braising dish on the stovetop over medium heat and add the oil. Season the short ribs with salt and pepper. Sear the meat on all sides until well browned. You may need to do this in batches to avoid overcrowding the pan. When done, remove each piece and set aside until all of the meat has been seared.

Add the onion, celery, carrot, and garlic to the pan and cook gently until softened and browned. Add the tomato paste to the vegetables, stir and then cook for another four minutes. Sprinkle the flour evenly over the vegetables. The mixture will become dry and clumpy in appearance. Add the wine and mix in well. Let this cook until it becomes very thick.

Return the short ribs to the braising pan and add just enough water to cover the meat. Add the thyme and bay leaves, and bring everything up to a boil. Then lower the temperature on the stovetop to low heat and bring the ribs to a slow simmer. Cover the pan and let cook for about three hours, or until the meat is fork tender. Alternatively, you could cook the ribs in a preheated 350°F oven for 2½ to three hours.

When ready, remove the meat from the braising pan. If the cooking sauce is too thin, place the braising dish on the stovetop over medium-high heat and gently boil the sauce until it has reduced and thickened to the desired consistency. Strain the sauce into a clean bowl, discarding the solids. If you are not serving immediately, store the ribs and sauce in the refrigerator until ready to use, or for up to three days.

Grilled Onglet (Hanger Steak)

Serves 6

Disclaimer: While a hanger steak is one of the most flavorful cuts on the animal, the kosher salting process makes this the second saltiest kosher cut of beef. Second only to the skirt steak, which is an inedible piece of garbage that I would never serve to any of my clients.

But just like the French don't pay attention to the skull and crossbones on the pack of cigs they adore so much, you should ignore this disclaimer also. A grilled hanger steak is a true treat that shouldn't be ruined for you by an overzealous rabbi with a bag of salt. Besides, as long as you don't salt it or add any kind of salty element to it (i.e., soy sauce), you will love this.

6 (8-ounce) hanger steaks,
butterflied open by your butcher

Coarsely ground black pepper
Peanut oil or canola oil

If you preheat and season the grill (page 112) and follow the same method for the grilling as in the recipe for Steak Frites (page 112), you will do very well for yourself. I find that when serving a hanger steak, a fresh and acidic element is a nice complement to clean up any residual salinity that may persist. A chimichurri sauce (page 124) or even just a squeeze of a fresh lemon will do the trick.

GRILLED STEAK FRITES

SERVES 6

6 (8-ounce) steak frites, cut
from the silvertip
Salt and coarse black pepper
Peanut oil or canola oil

6 portions homemade frites
(page 102), if you have the guts to
make them the Le Marais way)

Get that backyard grill good and hot, it usually takes at least 15 minutes until everything is smoking'.

Use a grill brush to scrub down the grill well and get rid of the remnants from your last attempt at grilling greatness that more than likely went as well as the last Hindenburg flight. Pieces of last weeks destroyed burgers are not a good complement to a steak frites.

[SIDENOTE: Have whatever sides you are serving with the steak ready to go before you cook the steaks on the grill. These steaks are thinly cut and will cook pretty damn fast.]

Lightly coat the steaks with oil and season them very well with salt and pepper.

Once you're ready to go, lay the steaks on to the grill. Leave them there, untouched, for about one minute before turning them 90 degrees on the same side to give you that groovy cross hatch pattern. Wait another minute and then flip them over and repeat on the other side for rare to medium-rare steaks.

For more cooked steak, leave them on the grill for an extra one minute per side for every temperature grade over medium-rare, flipping the steaks every so often to ensure even cooking and prevent burning.

PAN-SEARED RIB EYE STEAK

SERVES 6

Remove the rib eye steaks from the refrigerator and let them come to room temperature; this will take at least an hour. This step is vital to ensure an evenly cooked rib eye without that raw, cold spot in the middle. I can hear some of you whining already: Isn't that dangerous or unhealthy? It's fine as long as you are actually cooking the steak. Besides, the commies at the health department aren't in your kitchen looking for a bogus way to create fines in order to fill their coffers with ill-gotten booty the way they do with NYC restaurants.

3 (16-ounce) rib eye steaks	Kosher salt
Peanut oil or canola oil	Coarsely ground black pepper

Place a heavy-bottomed, 12-inch skillet on the stovetop over high heat and get it smoking hot. If you are the type who likes to destroy their beef, preheat an oven to 450°F.

Coat the steak lightly with your oil of choice, and season the heck out of both sides with salt and pepper. I'm being emphatic with the adjective for a reason. One of the biggest reasons why your steaks at home never taste as good as ours is that you are afraid to season the meat as generously as it needs to be. Now that I've shamed my mother with the cursing, let's move on.

Place a little bit of oil into the hot pan and then immediately place the steak in the center of the hot pan. Let the steak be for at least one minute before futzing with it. At this point, you should have a good browned char on the one side. If not, leave it be for another minute. Use tongs to turn the steak over and the repeat the process on the other side.

If cooking the steak to medium-rare, flip the steak back to its original side and the let it cook for another minute. Flip it back to the other side for another minute to get it to a rare to medium-rare temperature. Remove the steak from the pan and let it rest on a plate for at least six minutes before slicing into it.

If cooking above medium-rare, and why would you, slide the steak into a hot oven for an additional four minutes for every temperature grade above medium-rare.

TOURNEDOS ROSSINI

SERVES 8

Is there a combination of meat ingredients that are more indulgent than that of a tournedos of beef, foie gras, and black truffles? Ooff!!! I understand that you can't always get a piece of fresh foie; that's OK. The classic version of the dish uses a terrine de foie gras anyway. I adapted this recipe from one by Andre Soltner, the former chef of the New York classic Lutece. Extra Lipitor tonight!

Bread:

5 tablespoons (approximately ⅔ stick/⅓ cup) unsalted margarine

8 slices French bread, trimmed to the shape of the tournedos

Tournedos:

8 (5-ounce) tournedos of beef, room temperature

Salt and freshly ground black pepper

¼ cup extra virgin olive oil

Sauce:

1½ cups veal stock (page 2)

¼ cup truffle juice

4 teaspoons chopped black truffles

½ cup Madeira or sherry

3 tablespoons (approximately ⅓ stick) unsalted margarine

8 (2-ounce) slices foie gras terrine or mousse, room temperature

TO TOAST THE BREAD: Place a 10-inch skillet on the stovetop over medium heat and add the margarine. When the pan is hot, add the bread and quickly sauté the slices until browned on both sides. Remove the bread and set aside until ready to use.

TO COOK THE TOURNEDOS: Season the tournedos liberally with salt and pepper. Add the oil to the same skillet and raise the temperature on the stovetop to high. When the pan is hot, sear, or brown, the tournedos for three to four minutes per side for rare to medium-rare. Remove the meat from the pan and set aside while you make the sauce.

TO MAKE THE SAUCE: Place the veal stock, truffle juice, and truffles in a small bowl and mix to combine. Use a paper towel to wipe any excess fat from the pan, and place the skillet back on the stovetop over medium-high heat. Add the Madeira and deglaze the bottom of the pan. Add the veal stock mixture and bring to a boil. Remove the sauce from the heat and stir in the margarine to create a silky, smooth texture. Season with salt and pepper.

TO SERVE: Place one slice of toasted bread in the center of each plate. Top each with one tournedo and one slice of foie gras. Spoon the sauce over the top. If you have some extra truffle slices, use these for garnish.

PAN-SEARED TOURNEDOS OR STEAK AU POIVRE

SERVES 6

6 (8-ounce) tournedos or pepper steaks
Kosher salt
Coarsely ground black pepper
(tournedos only)

Peanut oil or canola oil
Au Poivre Sauce (page 7), if using

Remove the steaks from the refrigerator and bring them up to room temperature. I was very clear as to why in the rib eye recipe (page 114), so pay attention.

Place a heavy-bottomed, 12-inch skillet on the stovetop over high heat and get it smoking hot. If you are the type who likes to destroy their beef, preheat an oven to 450°F.

Coat the steak lightly with your oil of choice, and then season very well with the salt and pepper *only* if you are *not* making Steak au Poivre. If I have to tell you not to season the au poivre with pepper, then you should probably not be standing in front of an open flame or hot fire.

Place a little bit of oil into the hot pan and then immediately place the steak in the center of the hot pan. Let the steak be for at least one minute before futzing with it. At this point, you should have a good browned char on the one side. If not, leave it be for another minute. Use tongs to turn the steak over and repeat the process on the other side. Remove the steak from the pan and let it rest on a plate for at least eight minutes before slicing into it.

If cooking the steak to medium-rare or higher, slide the steak into a hot oven for an additional five minutes for every temperature grade above medium-rare.

Serve as is, or topped with au poivre sauce.

BRAISED BEEF CHEEKS

SERVES 8

Beef cheeks. In terms of pure flavor, texture, and richness, this is what I would call the foie gras of the steer. It's difficult to get your paws on, they are a special order for most butchers, but it's worth the effort and the wait. If the butcher tells you that you have to buy a large case, talk to those neighbors that you ordinarily don't want to or even the ones that creep you out, and arrange for the sharing of the case. You can go back to ignoring that neighbor after you get your cheeks, or at least until you need more.

5 tablespoons extra virgin olive oil

8 beef cheeks, trimmed of excess fat

Salt and freshly ground black pepper

2 medium-sized Spanish onions, peeled and cut into ¼-inch dice

1 medium-sized carrot, peeled and cut into ¼-inch dice

2 ribs celery, cut into ¼-inch

1 cup sherry

1 (28-ounce) can whole plum tomatoes, diced

3 cups rich brown veal stock (page 2)

1 fresh bay leaf

6 sprigs rosemary

Preheat the oven to 300°F.

Place an ovenproof, 6-quart, lidded braising dish on the stovetop over medium-high heat and add the oil. Season the beef very liberally with salt and pepper. When the pan is hot, sear, or brown, the cheeks very well on each side until a thick, richly browned crust has formed. You may need to do this in batches to avoid overcrowding the pan. Once all of the beef has been seared, set the pieces aside until ready to use.

Add the onions, carrots, and celery to the same pan with the rendered fat and cook, stirring occasionally, until they begin to brown and caramelize, about seven to nine minutes. Carefully pour the sherry into the pan to deglaze, stirring gently to loosen all the browned bits on the bottom of the pan. Lower the temperature on the stovetop to medium heat and cook until the liquid has reduced by half.

Return the beef cheeks back to the braising dish and add the tomatoes, rich brown veal stock, and herbs. Cover the dish with the lid and place it in the oven for about 3½ to four hours. When you insert a paring knife into the center of the meat and it comes out without any tension, and the meat is beginning to fall apart, the beef cheeks are done. Remove the meat from the pan and set aside to rest for at least 20 minutes before slicing.

Place the braising dish back on the stovetop over medium-high heat and bring to a boil. Cook until the liquid has reduced to a thickness of your liking. Strain the sauce into a clean bowl and season with salt and pepper.

Serve the beef cheeks with a starchy side dish such as egg noodles or pommes purée, or cool and store in their cooking liquid, covered, in the refrigerator; they will actually taste better after a few days rest. Gently reheat the beef cheeks, in the cooking liquid, in the oven before serving.

Bone-in Châteaubriand with Bordelaise Sauce

Serves 6

Classically, a Châteaubriand is made from the fat end of a beef tenderloin. This one of those rare occasions when not having access to a non-kosher cut works out for the better. The tenderloin of beef is a flavorless piece of meat with a mushy texture. Why it is so popular is a mystery to me. We take a dry-aged rib eye on the bone, and butcher it so that we can present a fillet on the bone.

Châteaubriand:

½ cup peanut oil

6 (18-ounce) bone-in Châteaubriand steaks

Salt and coarsely ground black pepper

Sauce:

2 cups dry red wine, such as cabernet sauvignon or Burgundy

2 medium-sized shallots, peeled and finely diced

6 sprigs thyme

1 fresh bay leaf

3 cups Demi-Glace (page 6)

Preheat the oven to 450°F.

TO MAKE THE CHÂTEAUBRIAND: Place a heavy-bottomed, 10-inch skillet on the stovetop over high heat and add the oil. Season the meat very liberally with salt and pepper and place it in the hot pan. Sear the steaks on both sides until a thick, richly browned crust has formed. You may need to do sear the meat in batches to avoid overcrowding the pan.

Place the steaks on a baking sheet and roast in the oven to the desired degree of doneness: approximately six minutes for medium-rare, eight minutes for medium, and 12 minutes for a medium-well to well-done steak. Remove the steaks from the hot pan and let rest on a platter for at least 10 minutes before slicing.

Place a 6-quart saucepan on the stovetop over high heat and add the red wine, shallots, thyme, and bay leaf. Bring this mixture to a boil and cook, boiling, until the wine has reduced to about ¼ cup. Add the demi-glace and continue to boil until the liquid has reduced by about half. Season the sauce with salt and pepper. Strain the sauce through a fine mesh strainer and into a clean bowl. Keep the sauce warm on the stovetop until ready to use.

When ready to serve the Châteaubriand steaks, run a sharp butcher's knife down along the side of the bone, separating the meat from the bone. Cut each Châteaubriand into ½-inch-thick slices. I like to give each guest the bone so that they can gnaw on it like a stray dog.

CHÂTEAUBRIAND WITH ROASTED BONE MARROW, PARSLEY, AND SHALLOTS

SERVES 6

Bone marrow is often referred to as meat butter. That's it for me, sold! Just like with our steaks at the restaurant, a little acidity in a salad works as the perfect contrast to the richness of the steak and marrow.

6 (3 to 4-inch long) large beef marrow bones

6 (18 to 20-ounce) bone-in Châteaubriand steaks

Salt and freshly ground black pepper

½ cup peanut oil

Parsley salad:

1 cup loosely packed flat leaf (Italian) parsley, leaves only

2 medium-sized shallots, peeled and thinly sliced

2 teaspoons capers, drained and coarsely chopped

2 teaspoons freshly squeezed lemon juice

Salt and freshly ground black pepper

2 tablespoons extra virgin olive oil

Preheat oven to 450°F.

TO MAKE THE BONE MARROW: Place the marrow, bone side up, in a 9 by 13-inch shallow roasting pan. Roast in the oven for 15 to 20 minutes until the marrow is soft and pulls away from the sides of the bone. Be careful to not over-roast the bones or the marrow will begin to ooze out.

TO MAKE THE CHÂTEAUBRIAND STEAKS: Place a heavy-bottomed, 10-inch skillet on the stovetop over high heat and add the oil. Season the meat very liberally with salt and pepper and place them in the hot pan. Sear the steaks on both sides until a thick, richly browned crust has formed. You may need to sear the meat in batches to avoid overcrowding the pan.

Place the steaks on a baking sheet and roast in the oven to the desired degree of doneness: approximately six minutes for medium-rare, eight minutes for medium, and 12 minutes for a medium-well to well-done steak. Remove the steaks from the hot pan and let rest on a platter for at least 10 minutes before slicing.

TO GARNISH AND SERVE: Place the parsley, shallots, capers, lemon juice, oil, salt and pepper in a bowl and toss to combine.

Place one Châteaubriand steak in the center of each plate. Spoon the marrow from the bones over the top of each steak. Garnish with a little bit of the parsley salad.

Grilled Rib eye Steak with Chimichurri Sauce and Fingerling Potato Salad

Serves 8 normal humans or 4 carnivorous beasts

Being that this big, fat ol' chunk of bovine flesh has been in the refrigerator for a long time, it is chilled to the bone. Pull it out of the refrigerator and leave it on the counter for about an hour before cooking time to let it come up to room temperature

This piece of meat is just too thick to be finished on your grill, so have your oven ready at 400 degrees.

2 (36-ounce) bone-in rib eye steaks
Salt and freshly ground black pepper
Peanut oil

Chimichurri sauce:

6 cloves garlic, peeled or 3 tablespoons roasted garlic purée
1 teaspoon red pepper flakes
3 teaspoons granulated sugar

½ cup apple cider vinegar
½ cup loosely packed, freshly chopped mint
½ cup loosely packed, freshly chopped flat leaf (Italian) parsley
½ cup loosely packed, freshly chopped basil
¾ cup extra virgin olive oil

Heat the grill to medium-high heat. Preheat the oven to 400°F.

If at this point your grill is not hot and well seasoned, you just have not been paying attention to a word that I have said anywhere in this book and you deserve to have your gorgeous and expensive beef stick to your grill.

Season the meat generously on all sides with salt and pepper. Place each steak directly on the hot grill and let it cook, untouched, for about five minutes. Don't play with your meat, this is the most common mistake made by home grillers. Use tongs to gently lift each steak off the grill and rotate it 90 degrees before gently placing it back on the grill, same side down; do not flip it over. This will create the desired diamond pattern. Grill for another three minutes and then flip the steaks over and repeat the process. Grill until you have a nicely browned char on both sides.

Place the meat on a baking sheet and roast in the oven for about 12 minutes. This should get you that perfect rare to medium-rare temperature this meat deserves. Above medium-rare? Hang your head in shame, you have disgraced the steer and made their existence meaningless. When the meat is cooked to your desired level of doneness, remove it from the oven and allow it to rest for 10 minutes before slicing.

Fingerling potato salad:

4 tablespoons Dijon mustard

2 tablespoons whole-grain mustard

2 tablespoons honey

6 tablespoons red wine vinegar

1 cup extra virgin olive oil

Salt and freshly ground black pepper

30 fingerling potatoes, par boiled in salted water (see page 137), and cooled

1 small red onion, peeled and thinly sliced

1 bunch watercress, rinsed and drained

¼ cup freshly chopped oregano

While the meat is cooking, prepare the sauce and the potato salad.

TO MAKE THE CHIMICHURRI SAUCE: Place all of the ingredients into the container of an electric blender, cover and process on medium speed until a coarsely textured, homogeneous sauce is formed. The sauce can be made up to eight hours in advance and stored in the refrigerator, well covered, until ready to use.

TO MAKE THE POTATO SALAD: Place both mustards, the honey, vinegar, and oil in a bowl and whisk to combine. Season with salt and pepper.

Slice the potatoes into bite-size pieces and place them in a bowl with the red onion, watercress, and the oregano. Toss with the dressing just before serving.

TO SERVE: Present these glorious cuts of beef on a cutting board, while wielding your sharp carving knife like a samurai warrior. Your guests will be thoroughly awed, and isn't that why we invite guests over in the first place?

Roasted Rib Eye, Fingerling Potatoes, and Haricot Vert

Serves 8

The mother of all holiday roasts. A massive hunk of glistening, fatty, beefy goodness. This is the payoff for having to spend time with that drunk uncle whom you keep the kids a safe distance away from. When deciding upon the level of doneness, remember that the ends will be more well done than the middle, allowing for both medium-rare and well-done pieces.

3 medium-sized carrots, peeled and cut into 2-inch lengths

2 medium-sized yellow onions, peeled and quartered

1 (6-pound) rib eye roast

Salt and freshly ground black pepper

Jus:

¾ cups dry, medium-bodied red wine, such as pinot noir or merlot

2 cups rich brown veal stock (page 2)

Salt and freshly ground black pepper

Potatoes:

2 pounds fingerling potatoes, scrubbed

Salt and freshly ground black pepper

4 tablespoons extra virgin olive oil

4 sprigs rosemary, leaves only, finely chopped

Haricot vert:

1 pound haricot vert, trimmed

3 tablespoons extra virgin olive oil

3 medium-sized shallots, peeled and thinly sliced

Preheat the oven to 450°F.

Place the carrots and onions in the bottom of a 9 by 13-inch shallow roasting pan and cover with 2 cups of water. Season the roast liberally with salt and pepper (that's a nice way of saying season the heck out of it) and place it on top of the vegetables. Roast the meat in the oven for 25 minutes to give it a crisp outer crust.

After 25 minutes, lower the oven temperature to 275°F and continue to roast for about another 45 minutes, or until the internal temperature of the roast reaches 130°F, which will yield a nice, medium-rare center. If you prefer your meat medium,

let it cook a little longer and remove it from the oven at an internal temperature of about 145°F. During the entire roasting process be sure to check the liquid level in the pan occasionally and add water, if necessary. You will need this liquid to make the *jus*.

When the roast is cooked to your liking, remove it from the pan and let it rest for 25 minutes before slicing. While the roast is cooling, finish the rest of the dish.

TO MAKE THE *JUS*: Strain the drippings from the roasting pan into a clean bowl, discarding the solids. Skim as much fat from the drippings as you can.

Place the same roasting pan on the stovetop over medium-high heat and return the skimmed drippings to the pan. Stir to deglaze and add in the wine and the rich brown veal stock. Bring to a boil and cook, stirring occasionally, until the liquid has reduced by one-third, about five minutes. Season with salt and pepper, and strain into a clean bowl.

TO MAKE THE POTATOES: Preheat the oven to 400°F. Place a baking sheet in the oven to preheat. Cut the potatoes to a size of your liking. I usually will either cut them in half or in thirds, depending on how big they are. Place the cut potatoes in a large bowl, season well with salt and pepper and toss with the oil and rosemary. Place the potatoes directly onto the hot baking sheet and roast in the oven until golden brown, about 20 minutes.

TO MAKE THE HARICOT VERT: Place a 4-quart saucepot filled with well-salted water over medium-high heat and bring to a boil. Add the beans and boil for about four minutes. You want the beans to be bright green and for the raw taste to be gone. When the beans are cooked to your liking, remove them from the pot and drain in a colander.

Place a 10-inch sauté pan on the stovetop over medium-high heat and add the oil. When the pan is hot, add the shallots and blanched beans and cook until heated through.

[SIDENOTE: If you are making the haricot vert in advance, remove them from the pot and immediately plunge them into a bowl of ice water to stop the cooking. Drain the beans and store in the refrigerator until ready to use, or for up to one day. Reheat and serve as directed above.]

My feeling on serving this dish is that family style is the only way to go. The roast, the potatoes and the beans should all be served in separate bowls with the *jus* in a traditional gravy boat. Very 1975.

WHOLE ROAST PRIME RIB OF BEEF

SERVES 12 TO 14

3 medium-sized carrots, peeled and cut into 2-inch lengths

2 medium-sized yellow onions, peeled and quartered

1 (12 to 14-pound) bone-in, dry-aged beef roast with 6 ribs

Salt and freshly ground black pepper

Jus:

¾ cups dry red wine, such as cabernet sauvignon or syrah

2 cups rich brown veal stock (page 2)

Salt and freshly ground black pepper

Preheat the oven to 450°F.

Place the carrots and onions in the bottom of a 9 by 13-inch shallow roasting pan and cover with 2 cups of water. Season the roast liberally with salt and pepper (that's a nice way of saying season the heck out of it) and place it on top of the vegetables. Roast the meat in the oven for 30 minutes to give it a crisp outer crust.

After 30 minutes, lower the oven temperature to 275°F and continue to roast for about another 45 minutes, or until the internal temperature of the roast reaches 130°F, which will yield a nice, medium-rare center. If you prefer your meat medium, let it cook a little longer and remove it from the oven at an internal temperature of about 145°F. During the entire roasting process be sure to check the liquid level in the pan occasionally and add water, if necessary. You will need this liquid to make the *jus*.

When the roast is cooked to your liking, remove it from the pan and let it rest for 25 minutes before slicing. While the roast is cooling, finish the rest of the dishes.

TO MAKE THE *JUS*: Strain the drippings from the roasting pan into a clean bowl, discarding the solids. Skim as much fat from the drippings as you can.

Place the same roasting pan on the stovetop over medium-high heat and return the skimmed drippings to the pan. Stir to deglaze and add in the wine and the rich brown veal stock. Bring to a boil and cook, stirring occasionally, until the liquid has reduced by one-third, about five minutes. Season with salt and pepper, and strain into a clean bowl.

When ready to serve, cut the meat in between the bones, slicing off six beautiful bone-in steaks. Serve with a generous portion of the *jus*.

Classics

Unless this is the first thing in the book that you have read, you know by now that I take great joy in making fun of the French. We do, however, have to stand up and give credit where it is due. The French have nailed food. Through their respect and appreciation for what the earth provides us, they have created not only great recipes and dishes, but an infectious food culture which I sure as hell hope that there is no cure for. So thank you to Marie-Antoine Careme and Auguste Escoffier. Thanks to Julia Child and Jacques Pepin. And thank you to Alain Ducasse and Jean-Georges Vongerichten. So many generations of great chefs that have sculpted the way that we eat. Without the French, life would be less delicious. (I just died a little.)

Salmon Coulibiac

Serves 8

There are a few givens in a kitchen. One is that if you bread or batter it and fry it, it always tastes good. Another is if you wrap it in puff pastry, it tastes good.

¾ cup wild rice

2 cups flat leaf (Italian) parsley, freshly chopped, divided

2 tablespoons (¼ stick / ⅛ cup) unsalted margarine

1 medium-sized leek, white part only, cleaned and thinly cut into 2-inch lengths

12 ounces fresh shitake mushrooms, stemmed and thinly sliced

Cooking spray

All-purpose flour, for dusting

1 (10 by 15-inch) sheet frozen puff pastry, thawed in the refrigerator

Salt and white pepper

1 (3-pound) salmon fillet, skinned and cleaned, all pin bones removed

2 large eggs, beaten

Crepes

1 cup all-purpose flour

Pinch of salt

3 eggs

2 cups nondairy coffee creamer

TO MAKE THE RICE: Place a 4-quart lidded saucepan on the stovetop over medium-high heat and add the rice, along with 2¼ cups of water. Season with salt and pepper. Cover the pan with the lid, and cook at a simmer until all of the water has been absorbed and the grains of rice have all opened up. Spread the rice onto on clean baking sheet to cool and sprinkle with 1 cup of the parsley.

TO MAKE THE MUSHROOMS: Place a 10-inch sauté pan on the stovetop over medium heat and add the margarine. When hot, add the leeks and cook gently until soft. Add the mushrooms and sauté until the mushrooms soften and begin to brown. Season with salt and pepper. Spread the vegetables onto on clean baking sheet to cool and sprinkle with the remaining parsley.

Preheat the oven to 400°F.

Line a baking sheet with a sheet of parchment paper and spray well with cooking spray. Lightly flour a clean work surface and lay the sheet of puff pastry in front of you lengthwise. Line three crepes down the center of the puff pastry. Spread the mushrooms out evenly in a line down the center of the crepes, the width and the length of the salmon fillet. Repeat the process with the wild rice.

Season the salmon with salt and pepper. Place the salmon top side down over the rice. Wrap the crepes up and around the salmon to enclose completely. If the crepes aren't large enough, use the remaining crepes to make up the difference, trimming off any excess. Repeat with the puff pastry, using extra puff pastry as needed to completely cover. Don't worry if it does not look pretty, as this will become the bottom of the coulibiac. Once well wrapped and trimmed of excess puff pastry dough, roll the coulibiac over and place it seam side down onto the prepared baking sheet.

Brush the entire coulibiac with the beaten egg. Place in the oven and bake until the dough is golden brown and crisp, about 30 minutes. A thermometer inserted into the center of the salmon should read 130°F.

Use a serrated knife to cut the coulibiac into slices and serve straight from the oven.

TO MAKE THE CREPES: Add the nondairy coffee creamer and the eggs to a bowl and whisk together. Add in the flour, salt and melted margarine. Whisk until smooth with the consistency of a thin pancake batter.

Bring a 10 inch, nonstick pan up to medium heat. Ladle in just enough batter to lightly coat the entire bottom of the pan. Tip the pan side to side to allow batter to spread as evenly as possible. Using a rubber spatula (or your fingertips if you're a real cook) to release the crepe from the pan and top turn it over. The crepe should be lightly browned on both sides. Reserve the crepe on a plate and repeat until you have at least 6 crepes. This can be done in advance and refrigerated overnight if need be.

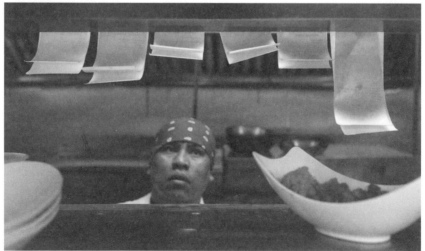

Bouillabaisse

Serves 8

There has been many an agreement among food nerds as to what exactly constitutes a true bouillabaisse. From what I know, and that's not much, a true bouillabaisse does not include shellfish, but the fish known as rascasse or scorpion fish. Working in a kosher environment, my vision may be skewed against lobster, but who cares? The recipe calls for either snapper or striped bass, assuming that you won't find the rascasse.

For this recipe you will need to start with whole red snapper and striped bass. Have your fishmonger dress, or scale and gut, each fish and fillet them into 3-ounce pieces, keeping the heads and bones separate.

4 pounds red snapper, scaled, gutted, and filleted into 3-ounce pieces, head and bones reserved. Your fishmonger can do this for you.

4 pounds striped bass, scaled, gutted, and filleted into 3-ounce pieces, head and bones reserved. If he's doing the snapper, the monger can do this for you as well.

Broth:

2 tablespoons extra virgin olive oil, plus extra for seasoning

2 medium-sized leeks, white part only, cleaned and thinly cut into 2-inch lengths

2 small Spanish onions, peeled, halved, and thinly sliced

1 medium fennel, bulb only, cleaned and thinly cut into 2-inch lengths

4 cloves garlic, peeled

3 fresh plum tomatoes, seeded and chopped

Reserved fish heads and bones (see header)

Peel of 2 oranges, white pith removed

4 sprigs flat leaf (Italian) parsley

1 small bunch tarragon

2 fresh bay leaves

¼ cup Sambuca (Pernod is preferable, but not kosher supervised)

Pinch saffron threads

Aioli garnish:

8 cloves garlic, peeled and roasted

Salt

5 saffron threads

1 large egg yolk

¼ cup extra virgin olive oil

Juice of 1 lemon

16 (¾-inch-thick) slices toasted baguette

Bouillabaisse:

8 Red Bliss potatoes, scrubbed

16 (3-ounce) pieces fresh red snapper (about 4 pounds)

16 (3-ounce) pieces fresh striped bass (about 4 pounds)

Salt and white pepper

TO MAKE THE BROTH: Place a 4-quart saucepan on the stovetop over medium heat and add the oil. When the pan is hot, add the leeks, onion, fennel, and garlic and let them sweat for about six minutes, until soft and translucent. Add the tomatoes and cook for another four to five minutes. Add the reserved fish heads and bones. Cook for about 10 minutes, stirring occasionally. Add the orange peel, parsley, tarragon, bay leaf, half of the Sambuca, and the saffron, and enough water to cover all of the ingredients. Lower the heat on the stovetop to low heat and simmer, uncovered, for about one hour. Remove the pan from the heat. Ladle the broth into a fine mesh strainer set over a clean bowl. Use the back of the ladle to push down against the solids to really extract as much of the liquid as possible. Discard the solids and hold the broth off to the side until ready to use.

TO MAKE THE AIOLI: Place the garlic and salt in the bowl of a food processor fitted with the blade attachment and process until smooth. Add the saffron and egg yolk and process until smooth. While the machine is running, slowly drizzle in the oil until you get an emulsified (think mayonnaise) consistency, adding the lemon juice at the very end. Because the lemon juice will thin the mix, you may need to add just a little more olive oil to bring the aioli back to a thicker consistency.

Remove the aioli and set aside until ready to serve if using it the same day. The aioli can be made one day in advance and stored covered in the refrigerator. Let the aioli come to room temperature before using.

TO FINISH THE BOUILLABAISE: Preheat the oven to 350°F.

Place a 4-quart saucepot on the stovetop over medium-high heat. Add the potatoes and enough water to cover the potatoes by one inch. Boil the potatoes until they are cooked nearly all the way through, about 25 minutes. You're going to finish cooking them with the fish, so only boil them until they are around three-quarters done. Submerge the potatoes in a bowl of ice water for four minutes to stop the cooking. Pat the potatoes dry and hold them in the refrigerator until ready to use.

Season each piece of fish with salt and pepper and place them along the bottom of a large, shallow casserole dish, being careful not to stack the pieces on top of one another. Cut the potatoes in half and arrange them among the pieces of fish.

Sprinkle the reserved broth with a generous amount of olive oil and the remaining Sambuca. Ladle the broth over the top of the fish to just barely cover. Cook in the oven for about eight minutes, or just until the fish has been cooked through.

Serve hot from the oven, with the aioli and toasted baguette served on the side. Encourage your guests to slather the garlicky aioli onto the croutons and dip them into the broth as they eat.

Coq au Vin

Serves 8

From the perspective of your everyday ugly American, I can understand why any recipe with a French title is intimidating. But just keep this in mind before shaking at the thought of producing one of these classic dishes. I have known many Frenchies in my life. None of them are all that complex. Many of their recipes are simple – case in point, the coq au vin. But this is a two-day process, so plan in advance.

All braised dishes can and should be made ahead of time; they always taste better the next day.

1½ (750-ml) bottles red wine, such as Burgundy or California cabernet

2 medium-sized Spanish onions, peeled and cut into ½–inch dice

2 medium-sized carrots, peeled, halved, and cut into ½–inch dice

2 stalks celery, halved and cut into ½–inch dice

8 whole cloves

1 tablespoon black peppercorns

12 sprigs thyme

2 fresh bay leaves

6 sprigs flat leaf (Italian) parsley

8 fresh chicken legs

8 fresh chicken thighs

Salt and freshly ground black pepper

4 to 5 tablespoons extra virgin olive oil, divided

3 tablespoons all-purpose flour

½ pound smoked veal bacon (optional), cut into a ½-inch dice

2 tablespoons (¼ stick/⅛ cup) unsalted margarine

20 pearl onions, peeled

1 pound white button mushrooms

Step One/Day One

Day one is a breeze. Place the wine, onions, carrots, celery, cloves, peppercorns, thyme, bay leaves, and parsley in a large bowl and mix to combine. Add the chicken, making sure that all of the pieces are fully submerged in the marinade. Cover the bowl with plastic wrap and refrigerate overnight.

Step Two/Day Two

Remove the chicken from the marinade and pat dry. Season the chicken on both sides with salt and pepper. Strain the marinade into a clean bowl, reserving the solids separately.

Place a large, lidded Dutch oven on the stovetop over medium-high heat and add 2 tablespoons of the oil. When the pan is hot, sear, or brown, the chicken pieces skin side down. Once the skin is fully browned, turn over and sear the meat side. If the skin sticks to the bottom of the pan when you try to turn it over, it's not done searing. Once all of the chicken has been seared, set aside until ready to use.

[SIDENOTE: You can be sure that if this is your first time searing meat, you will have sticking chicken. Don't sweat it, just keep moving on.]

Lower the temperature on the stovetop to medium heat, add the reserved solids to the pot and cook, stirring occasionally, until browned. Sprinkle the flour over the vegetables and mix well with a large spoon so that all of the vegetables are well coated. Stir in the reserved marinade. Bring the liquid to a boil, and return the browned chicken parts to the pot. Cover the pot and lower the temperature on the stovetop to low heat. Let cook, at a slow simmer, for about 1½ hours. The chicken is cooked through when the juice from the thigh runs clear when pierced.

While the chicken is stewing and you are polishing off the half bottle of wine left over from the recipe, begin the garnish. If using the bacon, and you should, place a 10-inch sauté pan on the stovetop over medium heat and 1 to 2 tablespoons of oil, just enough to barely coat the bottom of the pan. Add the bacon and cook until browned and crisp. Remove the bacon and drain on a paper towel.

Place a 4-quart saucepan on the stovetop over high heat, fill half full with water, add the margarine and bring to a boil. Add the pearl onions, lower the tem-perature to medium heat and cook until approximately three-quarters of the water has evaporated. Add the mushrooms and season with salt and pepper. Keep cooking until almost all of the water has evaporated, checking the vegetables for doneness. When ready, they should be tender and slightly browned. If they need more cooking time, add a bit more water and continue cooking as necessary.

Once the chicken is cooked, remove it from the stew and set aside. Check the consistency of the sauce; it should be thick enough to heavily coat the back of a spoon. If not, raise the temperature on the stovetop to medium-high and cook until the sauce has reduced to your desired level of thickness. Strain the sauce through a fine mesh sieve and into a clean bowl, discarding the solids. Season with salt and pepper.

This dish is best served over either mashed potatoes or egg noodles on a large platter. Artfully place the chicken legs and thighs on top of your starch of choice, and garnish with the bacon, onions and mushrooms, and sauce.

Duck a L'Orange

SERVES 2

I consider this be somewhat of an anomaly among the classic French dishes. Everyone and their grandmother is familiar with the name Duck a L'Orange, but most have never really had the true presentation of the dish. Not to mention that duck sometimes gets a bad rap as either gamey or too fatty. True, it's not as neutral as a commercially raised chicken, but it most certainly isn't gamey. When duck is properly cooked, the skin is like a ducky, crispy candy.

Duck:

1 fresh, whole duck (about 5½ pounds), trimmed of excess fat

Salt and white pepper

1 orange, quartered

1 lemon, cut into 6 pieces

Sauce a l'orange:

½ cup red wine vinegar

4 tablespoons granulated sugar

2 cups chicken stock (page 3), heated

⅓ cup Grand Marnier or Cointreau

2 teaspoons unsalted margarine

Zest of 2 oranges, finely zested

Juice of ½ orange

Juice of ½ lemon

Salt and white pepper

TO MAKE THE DUCK: Preheat the oven to 250°F.

Remove the giblets from the cavity of the duck. Rinse the duck inside and out thoroughly with cold water. Pat dry with a paper towel. Use a sharp knife to gently score the breasts with an X pattern. You want to score just the fat, not the flesh, so be careful not to cut too deep. Stuff the orange and lemon pieces into the cavity (I like to think of someone that I despise while I do this). Use kitchen twine to truss the duck like you would a chicken, with the legs tight up against the body. Also, cut off those wing tips, they tend to burn and get bitter.

[SIDENOTE: The purpose of scoring the duck is to help render out the fat, resulting in a crisp skin.]

Place the duck on a rack inside a 9 by 13-inch shallow roasting pan and cook in the oven for about 30 minutes. At this point the duck won't have much, if any, color. However, there should be rendered duck fat in the bottom of the roasting pan. Remove the bird from the oven and let it cool in the pan to room temperature.

Raise the oven temperature to 350°F. Place the duck back into the oven and roast for an additional 60 minutes. During this process, the duck will render out much of its fat into the bottom of the pan, leaving a skin that is well browned and crispy.

[SIDENOTE: About halfway through the roasting step, check the duck for signs of browning. Many ovens have hot spots and you may need to rotate the bird to ensure even browning.]

Once the duck is cooked, remove the pan from the oven. Lift the duck and the rack from the roasting

pan and set aside. Carefully pour off the duck fat and juices from the pan and into a clean container. Save this; you can cool it and use it for anything from making duck confit to frying potatoes. I charge a lot of money for this stuff, so make good use of it! Set the roasting pan aside, as is, until ready to finish the sauce a l'orange.

TO MAKE THE SAUCE A L'ORANGE: While the duck is roasting, place a 2-quart saucepan on the stovetop over high heat. Add the vinegar and sugar and bring to a boil. Use a wet pastry brush to brush down the inside of the pan to prevent the sugar from crystalizing and burning. Cook until the sugar mixture turns a light caramel color. Slowly and carefully add the hot chicken stock. Be warned, the sugar is unbelievably hot, and if you add the stock too quickly it will boil up and may burn you. I warned you, so no whining after the fact. Lower the temperature on the stovetop to low heat and simmer for about 45 minutes. The sauce should have reduced by about half at this point.

Place the roasting pan on the stovetop over medium heat and very carefully add the Grand Marnier to deglaze the pan. Another warning, this stuff has a high alcohol content and will catch fire easily. Don't want to lose those eyebrows or lengthy beards now do we. Use a wooden spoon to scrape all the browned bits from the bottom of the pan. Cook, stirring occasionally, until most of the alcohol has cooked off, about four minutes. Pour this mixture into the simmering sauce. Continue to simmer until the sauce has again reduced by half, then strain it through a fine mesh strainer into a clean saucepan, discarding any solids. Place the saucepan on the stovetop over low heat and bring the sauce back up to a simmer. Whisk in the margarine, then add the orange zest, and orange and lemon juices. Simmer until the sauce

has reduced to the desired consistency; it should be thick enough to coat the back of a spoon. Season with salt and pepper.

TO CARVE THE DUCK: Once you have hopefully not dishonored the life of the bird by destroying it, let's break it down into recognizable parts.

1. Remove the bird from the roasting pan and place it breast-side up on a clean carving board. Allow the bird to rest for at least 10 minutes before you begin.

2. First, loosen the legs by cutting the skin between the thigh and the breast with the tip of your knife. Then pull the thighs away from the breast down toward the cutting board one at a time. Then find the joint where the thighbone connects to the body and cut straight down to remove the leg.

3. Once the legs have been removed, place them skin-side down on the cutting board. Find the joint that connects the leg and the thigh, and cut down directly onto it. Repeat with the other leg and then place them onto the serving dish.

4. To remove the breast from the body, cut down on either side of the breastbone until you feel the resistance from the cartilage beneath. Using the cartilage as your guide, run your knife down either side of the bird until the breast is separated. Repeat on the other side of the bird.

5. Save the carcass in the freezer for stocks.

To serve, I like to pour some of the sauce onto the bottom of a platter and then artfully arrange the carved duck over the sauce. What's the point of going through the process of crisping up the skin if I'm going to mush it up with sauce? . Strange as it may seem, a 5½ pound duck will only feed two normal diners. On a good day, this will feed only me.

Cassoulet

Serves 8

The cassoulet is considered the one of the signature dishes of the south of France, particularly in Toulouse, Carcassonne, and Castelnaudary. The dish is name for the traditional cooking vessel that it is cooked in, a cassoulet.

Modern chefs who feel the need to improve upon what doesn't need to be improved, have tried many haute cuisine versions of the cassoulet. I suppose the goal was to make it with less fat and all of the flavor. All these attempts have, in my opinion (and who else's opinion really matters?!), fallen short in their misguided attempts. Let's face it, this is a dish that will be eaten at most a few times a year. It is perfect as it is. Rich, creamy, and a bit salty. Indulge.

In the spirit of full disclosure, this is a three-day process. Each step is easier than the next, yet, the time frame is unavoidable. For what it's worth, this is the perfect Shabbos dish, it destroys any cholent ever made.

Duck confit:

8 fresh duck legs, skin on

Coarse sea salt

3 cups duck fat

Freshly ground black pepper

12 sprigs thyme

3 sprigs rosemary

4 cloves garlic, peeled

Cassoulet:

6 cups dried white beans such as Tarbais, Great Northern, or butter beans

3 pounds fresh or smoked veal breast (I prefer smoked), cut into 1½-inch cubes

1 medium-sized Spanish onion, peeled and quartered

1 small bunch rosemary

2 fresh bay leaves

4 cloves garlic, peeled and thinly sliced

1 small bunch flat leaf (Italian) parsley

Salt and freshly ground black pepper

½ cup duck fat, melted

8 large veal sausages

4 medium-sized Spanish onions, peeled and cut into a ¼-inch dice

8 duck confit legs

Optional topping:

1½ cups dry bread crumbs

¼ cup chopped fresh flat leaf (Italian) parsley

Day One

TO START THE CONFIT: Rub the duck legs generously with salt and place them side-by-side in a shallow dish. Cover the dish with plastic wrap and refrigerate overnight.

TO START THE CASSOULET: Place the beans in a large bowl and add enough cold water to the cover the beans by three inches. Cover the bowl with plastic wrap and refrigerate overnight.

Day One is done. So far, so easy.

Day Two

TO MAKE THE CONFIT: Preheat the oven to 350°F. Place a 1-quart saucepan on the stovetop over medium-high heat and add the duck fat. Heat the fat until melted and hot. Season the duck legs with pepper. Place the legs in a shallow, ovenproof baking dish along with the thyme, rosemary, and garlic. Carefully pour the hot, melted duck fat into the dish to cover the legs. Cover the dish with foil and cook in the oven for approximately one hour. When ready, the meat should be tender and the skin should pull away from the knuckle at the end of the leg.

Remove the dish from the oven and allow the duck to cool, untouched, in the refrigerator overnight.

TO MAKE THE CASSOULET: Drain and rinse the soaked beans. Place a 4-quart saucepot on the stovetop over medium-high heat and add the beans, veal breast, onion, rosemary, bay leaves, and garlic. Cover the mixture with water, season with salt and pepper, and bring to a boil. Lower the temperature on the stovetop to low heat and cook at a simmer until the beans are tender, possibly up to one hour.

Remove the pot from the heat and set the veal breast aside until ready to use. Discard the herbs and onion, and allow the beans to cool in the cooking liquid to room temperature. Strain the cooking liquid into a clean bowl and set it and the beans aside separately until ready to use.

Preheat the oven to 350°F.

Place a 10-inch sauté pan on the stovetop over medium heat and add 1 tablespoon of duck fat. Add the sausages and brown them on all sides. Once browned, drain on paper towel and set aside until ready to use. Place the onions and garlic in the same hot pan and cook in the rendered fat until browned.

Layer one-third each of the beans and onion mixture in a large, ovenproof dish. Add all of the sausages and about half of the duck fat. Cover with another one-third each of beans and onion mixture, all of the veal breast, and the duck legs. Last but not least come the remaining beans, onion mixture, and duck fat. Pour in enough of the reserved cooking liquid to just cover the beans. Cook in the oven for one hour, then lower the oven temperature to 225°F and cook for another hour. Remove from the oven, cool and refrigerate overnight.

This concludes Day Two of our program. A bit more involved, yet no reason to call in Paul Bocuse for back up.

Day Three

Preheat the oven to 350°F.

Place the bread crumbs and parsley in a bowl and mix to combine. Sprinkle the bread-crumb topping over the entire top of the dish.

[SIDENOTE: You can certainly omit this step. Depending on your school of thought, some will insist you skip this and others, like myself, think that it's a must. Whatever floats your boat, mine almost always floats better with a crispy crust.]

Bake the cassoulet in the oven for approximately 45 minutes to one hour, just until the center is as hot as the surface of the sun. Don't try to be cute when serving. Cassoulet may not look like a work of art, but I guarantee that it will taste like it belongs in the Louvre.

We made it through! Celebrate with a huge glass of red wine and a pile of Cassoulet.

PETIT SALE

SERVES 8

This is a very popular winter dish in France. Like all great French dishes, it's best served with a crunchy French baguette and a sturdy bottle of Burgundy. Just be careful to not ruin your meal by dining with an actual Frenchman.

¼ cup extra virgin olive oil

4 (4 to 5-inch long) smoked veal sausages

12 ounces smoked veal bacon, either a whole slab or thick slices

8 duck confit legs (page 36)

4 ribs celery, cut into ½ inch dice

4 medium-sized carrots, peeled and cut into ½-inch dice

1 large Spanish onion, peeled and cut into ½-inch dice

1 leek, white part only, cleaned and thinly cut into 2-inch lengths

4 cloves garlic, peeled and coarsely chopped

1 (16-ounce) box dry French green lentils

2 fresh bay leaves

6 sprigs rosemary

4 cups chicken stock (page 3), or water

Salt and freshly ground black pepper

Place a heavy-bottomed, 6-quart lidded casserole dish on the stovetop over medium heat and add the olive oil. Slice the sausages in half lengthwise, place them in the hot oil, and brown on all sides. Remove the sausages from the pan and repeat the browning process with the bacon and the duck legs. Drain the meat on paper towel until ready to use.

Add the celery, carrots, onion, leeks, and garlic to the same pan and cook until caramelized, about eight minutes. Season with salt and pepper. Add the lentils, bay leaves, and rosemary. Pour in the chicken stock, bring everything to a boil, and then lower the temperature on the stovetop to low heat and bring to a simmer. Add the meat to the pot, cover, and let simmer until the lentils are tender; this will take at least 40 minutes.

When ready to serve, check the seasoning and spoon some of the stew into each bowl. Top each bowl with one duck leg, one piece of sausage, and a few slices of bacon. Huge hunks of bread are a must for sopping up all of the smoky, fatty juices.

Pot au Feu

It may be time for a little honesty on my part. I'm not a huge fan of the frogs from across the pond. We all have our own feelings and preconceived notions about the French, the majority of these are true. I am, for what it's worth, the ugliest of all ugly Americans and wear that badge with tremendous pride. This dish knocks out of the park the concept that all French food is overly complicated. If you can chuck a bunch of stuff into a pot and let it simmer, you can make Pot au Feu.

1½ pounds beef paleron (see page 109), or brisket

8 pieces oxtail, cut into 1½-inch pieces

8 pieces beef short ribs

2 veal shanks

8 cloves garlic, peeled

2 small Spanish onions, peeled and halved

7 medium-sized leeks, white part only, cleaned

1 large or 2 small celery roots, peeled and quartered

4 medium-sized carrots, peeled and cut into 3-inch lengths

1 bouquet garni (5 sprigs thyme, 5 sprigs rosemary, 5 sprigs parsley, and 2 fresh bay leaves all tied together with butcher's twine or in a piece of cheesecloth)

Salt and freshly ground black pepper

4 medium-sized potatoes, peeled and halved

1 head green cabbage, cored and cut into 8 wedges

Sea salt

¾ pound drained cornichons

1½ cups Dijon mustard

Place a 6½-quart braising pan on the stovetop over medium-high heat. Add the paleron, oxtail, short ribs, and veal shank, along with enough water to completely cover all of the meat, and bring to a boil. As soon as the mixture comes to a boil, remove the pan from the heat. Strain out all of the water, keeping the meat in the pan. Place the pan back on the stovetop over medium-high heat, and add the garlic, onion, leek, celery root, carrot, and the bouquet garni. Season well with salt and pepper. Add enough cold water to completely cover all of the ingredients, and bring everything to a simmer. Lower the temperature on the stovetop to low heat and cook, simmering, for about three hours, until all of the meat is tender. Skim the surface of the liquid every now and then to remove any foam or scum. After three hours, add the potatoes and the cabbage and cook for an additional 30 minutes, or until the potatoes are soft. Taste the broth as you go for any necessary seasoning adjustments.

I like to remove the paleron from the broth and slice it into workable hunks. Remove the meat from the veal shanks, the short ribs and the oxtail as well. Do your best to arrange the serving platter so that everyone gets a little piece of each type of meat.

Put the vegetables on the same platter with the meat, and sprinkle everything with some of the sea salt. I like to keep the broth in a gravy boat for easy serving. I also find that using bowls instead of plates is the way to go, so your guests can sop up some of that gloriously unctuous broth with a hunk of bread.

The cornichon and the Dijon mustard should be placed on the table for your guests.

Unpretentious, simple, and an absolute pleasure, as un-French as it gets!

BAECKEOFFE

SERVES 8

The classic Shabbos meal is the cholent. It's about time to try something a little different. This is a dish that comes from the north of France, with obvious German influence. The story behind this is that the women would prepare this dish on Sunday evening and leave it with the baker to slowly cook in his gradually cooling oven on Monday while they headed down to the river to wash the families' clothes. The baker would seal the casserole with his leftover dough. The women would pick up the casserole along with a loaf of bread. I can't verify this, but it's a good story. This recipe is adapted from the Alsatian chef Hubert Keller.

Marinade:

2 medium-sized Spanish onions, peeled and cut into ¼-inch dice

2 small leeks, white and tender green parts only, cleaned and thinly cut into 2-inch lengths

2 small carrots, peeled and thinly cut into 2-inch lengths

3 cloves garlic, peeled and sliced

1 teaspoon juniper berries

4 sprigs thyme

3 tablespoons freshly chopped flat leaf (Italian) parsley

3 cups dry riesling

1 pound beef paleron (see page 109), cut into 1¼-inch cubes

1 pound lamb shoulder, trimmed, cut into 1¼-inch cubes

1 pound veal breast, trimmed and cut into 1¼-inch cubes

Baeckoffe:

Extra virgin olive oil

3 pounds large Yukon Gold potatoes, peeled and cut crosswise into ⅛-inch-thick slices

Salt and freshly ground black pepper

Pastry seal:

¾ cup all-purpose flour

5 tablespoons cold water

1 tablespoon extra virgin olive oil

1 large egg, beaten

TO MAKE THE MARINADE: Combine the onions, leeks, carrots, garlic, juniper berries, thyme, parsley, and wine in a large bowl. Add all of the meat to the marinade, cover the bowl with plastic wrap and refrigerate overnight. Make sure that the meat remains submerged in the marinade the entire time.

TO MAKE THE BAECKOFFE: Preheat the oven to 350°F.

Remove the meat from the marinade. Strain the vegetables from the marinade and set all aside.

Evenly coat the bottom of an ovenproof, 6-quart lidded casserole dish with oil.

Layer half of the potato slices in the bottom of the dish. Arrange the meat over the potatoes, followed by the vegetables. Top with the remaining potato slices, and then cover with the reserved marinade.

While there should be enough liquid to just cover the potatoes, if needed add some additional wine or water. Season with salt and pepper.

TO MAKE THE PASTRY SEAL: Place the flour, water, and oil in a bowl and mix together by hand until the dough holds together. Turn the dough out onto a lightly floured work surface and gently roll it into a rope long enough to wrap around the rim of your casserole dish. Gently press the rope in place against the rim. Firmly cover the casserole dish with the lid,

pressing the dough in place and creating the seal. Use a pastry brush to brush the exposed dough rope with the egg. Up to this point, the Baeckoffe can be made one day in advance and stored in the refrigerator.

Place the covered casserole dish in the oven for about 3½ hours. Remove the Baeckoffe from the oven and let it rest slightly before serving. Bring the Baeckoffe to the dinner table and use a chef's knife to cut the baked dough from the outside of the casserole dish. Remove the lid and serve.

BEEF BOURGUIGNON

SERVES 6

I don't think that anyone would disagree that this dish is the mother of all classic dishes in French cuisine. It encompasses all the basics: easy to prepare, lots of red wine, and an unsavory cut of beef. Don't be intimidated by the snooty French name and pronunciation, it's only a pot roast. A damn tasty pot roast, but none the less, a pot roast.

My personal preference for the cut of beef is the paleron. also known as the chicken steak. An equal volume of a shoulder or neck would do just as well.

---

3 pounds beef paleron (see page 109), cut into 1½-inch cubes

Salt and freshly ground black pepper

Extra virgin olive oil

4 medium-sized Spanish onions, peeled and cut into ½-inch dice

6 medium-sized carrots peeled and cut into 1-inch lengths

4 ribs celery, cut into 1-inch lengths

4 cloves garlic, peeled and thinly sliced

4 tablespoons all-purpose flour

3 tablespoons tomato paste

1 (750 ml) bottle red Burgundy, or any other full-bodied red wine

1 small bunch thyme

2 fresh bay leaves

4 cups rich brown veal stock (page 2)

Place a 6-quart, lidded Dutch oven on the stovetop over high heat and coat the bottom with oil. When the oil begins to slightly smoke, the pan is hot enough to properly sear, or brown, the meat.

Season the meat liberally with salt and pepper. Working in batches, sear the meat on all sides until *well* browned. Not grayish to browned, *well* browned. When done, remove each piece and set aside until all of the meat has been seared.

[SIDENOTE: The reason that we sear the meat in batches is to the prevent overcrowding in the pan, which impacts the ability to fully brown or sear.]

Lower the temperature on the stovetop to medium heat. Add the onions, carrots, celery, and garlic to the same Dutch oven with all of the browned bits and pieces. Cook for about 10 minutes, stirring occasionally, until the vegetables begin to brown. Stir in the tomato paste and cook for another three minutes. Sprinkle the flour over the vegetables and mix well with a large spoon so that all of the vegetables are well coated. Add the wine. Use a wooden spoon to scrape up all of the bits and nubbins on the bottom of the pot, and bring everything to a rolling boil.

Return all of the seared meat to the Dutch oven. Use kitchen twine to tie together the thyme and the bay leaves and then add them to the pot. Add the rich brown veal stock. If all of the ingredients are not fully submerged, add just enough water to cover. Lower

the heat on the stovetop to low temperature and bring the stew to a slow simmer. Let it cook for about two hours, covered, or until the meat is fork tender.

[SIDENOTE: While the stew is cooking I like to give it a stir and bottom scraping every 20 or so minutes, just to make sure that nothing is sticking to the bottom of the pan and burning. If there is, chances are that either the heat is on too high or the liquid is too thick. Don't be afraid to add more water if needed.]

Before serving, skim the top of the stew of any excess fat or scum collecting on the surface. Taste the broth for any seasoning adjustments and serve.

Lamb

Lamb is a delicious, protein-packed meat that we should all be eating more often than just at the holidays or on special occasions. It seems that price is a major component in buyers' preference of beef over lamb. Beef production per pound in the U.S. is 1600 times that of U.S. lamb production. Basic supply and demand at play here.

LAMB NAVARIN

SERVES 8

Lamb Navarin is one of those dishes that brings me back to skills classes at the CIA (Culinary Institute of America). I recall making a series of small incisions in my thumb while trying to perfect the turning of vegetables into little football shapes.

Lamb:

4 tablespoons extra virgin olive oil

4 pounds lamb shoulder and neck, cut in 1-inch cubes

Salt and freshly ground black pepper

1 medium-sized carrot, peeled and cut into ¼-inch dice

2 medium-sized Spanish onions, peeled and chopped

2 cloves garlic, peeled and sliced

2 tablespoons tomato paste

3 tablespoons instant all-purpose flour

Vegetables:

5 medium-sized carrots, peeled and cut into 1½-inch long pieces

5 medium-sized parsnips, peeled and cut into 1½-inch long pieces

8 fingerling potatoes, halved lengthwise

6 tablespoons (¾ stick / 3 ounces) unsalted margarine

3 tablespoons honey

24 pearl onions, peeled

1 cup frozen peas

1 cup flat leaf (Italian) parsley, coarsely chopped, to garnish

Preheat the oven to 350°F.

TO MAKE THE LAMB: Place a 6-quart, lidded Dutch oven on the stovetop over high heat and add the oil. When the oil begins to slightly smoke, the pan is hot enough to properly sear the meat.

Season the lamb liberally with salt and pepper. Working in batches, sear the meat on all sides until *well* browned. You may need to do this in batches to avoid overcrowding the pan. When done, remove each piece and set aside until all of the meat has been seared.

Add the carrot and onion to the same Dutch oven used to sear the lamb. Cook the vegetables, stirring occasionally, until they are soft and well browned.

Add the garlic and the tomato paste, stir, and then cook until the tomato paste begins to brown, about four minutes. Sprinkle the flour evenly over the vegetables, stir, and cook for about another four minutes.

Return the lamb to the pan and add enough water to cover the meat. Cover the pan, place in the oven and cook until the lamb is tender. This may take anywhere between one and 1½ hours. When ready, use a slotted spoon to transfer the lamb to a plate and set aside.

Place the Dutch oven back on the stovetop over high heat and cook until the sauce has reduced down to about 3 cups. At this point the sauce should be thick

enough to coat the back of a spoon. Strain the sauce into a large saucepan, discarding the solids. Set the sauce aside until ready to reheat and serve.

TO MAKE THE VEGETABLES: Place an 8-inch lidded skillet on the stovetop over medium-high heat and add the carrots, parsnips, fingerling potatoes, margarine, honey, salt, and 2 cups of water. Partially cover and cook for 10 minutes. Add the pearl onions, partially cover and continue cooking until the liquid has evaporated and the vegetables are tender,

about 10 minutes more. Uncover and continue to cook, stirring, until the vegetables are golden brown, about three minutes. Add 2 tablespoons of water, toss in the peas, stir to glaze the vegetable, and then remove from the pan from stovetop.

TO SERVE: Place the sauce-filled saucepan on the stovetop over low to medium heat. Warm the sauce until hot and stir in the meat and vegetables. Divide the stew evenly between dishes and garnish with parsley.

LAMB COUSCOUS

SERVES 8

2 pinches saffron threads

6 tablespoons (¾ stick/ 3 ounces) unsalted margarine, divided

3 tablespoons extra virgin olive oil

2 medium-sized Spanish onions, peeled and thinly sliced

8 (10 to 12-ounce) lamb shanks

Salt and freshly ground black pepper

2 tablespoons paprika, divided

4 teaspoons ground cumin

1 teaspoon ground cayenne pepper

1 (28-ounce) can plum tomatoes, drained and diced

13 sprigs flat leaf (Italian) parsley, 3

sprigs thyme and 1 bay leaf tied together with cheesecloth

5 ribs celery, cut into 1½-inch lengths

3 large carrots, peeled and cut into 1½-inch lengths

3 medium-sized zucchini, cut into 1½-inch lengths

1½ cups whole almonds, blanched

1½ cups pitted Kalamata olives

4 cups couscous

½ cup loosely packed mint leaves, freshly chopped

1 cup prepared or store-bought harissa, for serving on the side

Place the saffron in a small bowl and cover with 4 teaspoons of hot water. Let sit, untouched, for at least 10 minutes.

Place a 6-quart, lidded Dutch oven on the stovetop over medium heat and add 4 tablespoons of the margarine and the oil. When melted and hot, add the onion. Cook, stirring occasionally, until softened but not browned, about four to five minutes. Remove the onion from the pan and set aside.

Season the lamb shanks with salt, pepper, and half of the paprika. Add the shanks to the Dutch oven and sear the meat on all sides until well browned. When done, remove each piece and set aside until all of the meat has been seared.

Add the cumin, cayenne, and the remaining paprika to the rendered fat in the bottom of the pan and cook, stirring, for about 1 minute. Add the toma-

toes, onions, and lamb shanks, and enough water to cover the meat by about three-quarters. Raise the temperature on the stovetop to high heat and bring everything to a boil. Lower the temperature on the stovetop to low heat. Bring to a simmer and skim off any fat from the surface of the broth. Add the saffron and its soaking liquid, the tied up herbs and season with salt and pepper. Partially cover the pan and simmer until the lamb is tender, about 2½ to three hours. When tender, transfer the lamb shanks to a large plate and set aside to slightly cool.

To the still-simmering broth, add the celery and carrots. Cover the pan and continue to simmer until the vegetables are almost tender, about 10 minutes. You may need to raise the temperature on the stovetop to medium heat. Add the zucchini, almonds, and olives and simmer another 10 minutes until all of the vegetables are tender. Remove the pan from the stovetop and take out the herb bundle. Measure out 2 cups of the cooking liquid and set this aside.

Once the lamb shanks have cooled enough to handle, remove the meat from the bone and coarsely shred it by hand. Discard the bones and return the meat to the Dutch oven and the remaining broth and vegetables.

TO PREPARE THE COUSCOUS: Place a 2-quart, lidded saucepan on the stovetop over medium-high heat and add the remaining 2 tablespoons margarine. When melted, add the couscous and cook, stirring, until the couscous is slightly toasted, about four minutes. Stir in 4 cups of water, the reserved 2 cups cooking liquid, salt and pepper and bring to a boil. Cover the pan, remove it from the heat, and let sit, untouched, until the couscous has absorbed all of the liquid, about 10 to 12 minutes. Fluff the couscous with a fork.

Just before serving, check the lamb stew for seasoning. To serve, make a mound of couscous on a platter and then generously ladle the lamb stew over the mound. Garnish with mint and serve with a nice, spicy harissa on the side.

BRAISED LAMB SHANKS

SERVES 8

I'm not sure that there is any dish that is better suited for a cold winter day than braised lamb shanks. Like all braised dishes, they are deceptively simple to make and make for great leftovers. Great for one of those days when the entire family is home, unshowered, lounging in their pajamas. I serve this with my personal favorite side dish of creamy polenta, though any absorbent starch will do the trick.

4 tablespoons peanut oil	Pinch saffron threads
8 (12 to 14-ounce) lamb shanks	5 sprigs mint, plus extra for garnish
Salt and white pepper	
2 medium-size yellow onions, peeled and thinly sliced	5 sprigs rosemary
4 cloves garlic, peeled	1 cinnamon stick
2 tablespoons tomato paste	4 cardamom pods
1 cup all-purpose flour	1 teaspoon fennel seeds
1 (750-ml) bottle dry red wine, such as Bordeaux	1 teaspoon cumin seeds
	1 teaspoon pink peppercorns
3 fresh plum tomatoes, seeded and diced	Rind of 1 orange
2 large carrots, peeled and cut into ¼-inch dice	8 dried figs
	8 dried apricots

Preheat the oven to 300°F.

Place a 14 by 17-inch lidded braising dish on the stovetop over medium-high heat and add the oil. Season the lamb shanks with salt and pepper. Working in batches, sear the meat on all sides until *well* browned. When done, remove each piece and set aside until all of the lamb has been seared.

Add the onions and garlic to the pan and cook until the onions are well caramelized. Add the tomato paste, stir, and cook until the tomato paste begins to brown, about three minutes. Sprinkle the flour evenly over the vegetables, stir and cook for about another four minutes. Add the wine and mix in well. Use a spoon to scrape off all of the fond from the bottom of the pan. Reduce the temperature on the stovetop to medium heat and cook until the liquid thickens, about three to four minutes.

Return the lamb to the pan and add the tomatoes, carrots, and saffron. Pour in just enough water to cover the meat. Place the remaining herbs, spices, and the orange rind in a cheesecloth bag, tie closed and then drop that into the pan. Cover the pan and place in the oven for about three hours. At the 2½ hour mark add the figs and apricots. Cook for another 30 minutes, or until tender.

When fully cooked, remove the lamb from the pan serve in a bowl with some of the onions, tomato, carrots, and dried fruits. Garnish with fresh mint.

Slow-Roasted Lamb Shoulder Roast with Flageolets

Serves 8

*F*lageolets are best known for their role in Cassoulet. They are however, traditionally served with lamb, as in this dish. The inspiration for this dish came from the chef Jean-Michel Diot from his days at the old-school, classic French bistro Park Bistro. He is now the chef/owner of Tapenade restaurant in La Jolla, California. This would do very well served with the braised fennel, apples, and onions (page 223).

Lamb:

3 tablespoons vegetable oil

1 (4-pound) lamb shoulder roast

Salt and freshly ground black pepper

2 medium-sized Spanish onions, peeled and cut into ¼-inch dice

1 large carrot, peeled and cut into ¼-inch dice

1 rib celery, coarsely chopped

½ cup tomato paste

1 cup all-purpose flour

1 (750-ml) bottle dry red wine, such as a merlot or pinot noir

1 cheesecloth bag with the following spices: 1 kaffir lime leaf, ½ teaspoon cumin seed, 1 teaspoon minced fresh ginger root, ½ teaspoon black peppercorns, ¼ teaspoon whole all spice, 3 whole cloves

Beans:

1 pound dried flageolet beans

3 tablespoons extra virgin olive oil

1 medium-sized Spanish onion, peeled and cut into ¼-inch dice

1 medium-sized carrot, peeled and cut into ¼-inch dice

2 ribs celery, cut into ¼-inch dice

4 cloves garlic, peeled and sliced

3 cups vegetable broth

1 fresh bay leaf

3 sprigs rosemary

Salt and freshly ground black pepper

Garnish:

1 cup dried apricots

1 cup dried figs, halved lengthwise

1 bunch mint

TO MAKE THE LAMB: Preheat the oven to 325°F.

Place a 6-quart braising pan on the stovetop over medium-high heat and add the oil. Generously season the lamb with salt and pepper. When the pan is hot, add the lamb, fat side down, and sear until you get a deep brown color. Use a pair of tongs to flip over the roast and cook until seared on all sides. When done, remove the roast from the pan and set aside.

Add the onions, carrot, and celery to the same pan used to sear the lamb. Cook the vegetables, stirring occasionally, until they are soft and well browned. Add the tomato paste, stir, and then cook until the tomato paste begins to brown, about four minutes.

[SIDENOTE: Cooking the tomato paste for a few minutes removes the raw tomato paste flavor, and also increases its thickening power in the sauce.]

Sprinkle the flour evenly over the vegetables, stir, and cook for another two minutes. Add the wine and mix well to combine. The mixture should begin to thicken immediately. Return the lamb roast to the pan and then add enough water to come about one-quarter of the way up the roast. Bring everything to a boil, then lower the temperature on the stovetop to low heat and bring to a simmer. Place the braising pan in the oven and cook the roast for three hours, until you can easily insert and remove the blade of a knife into the center of the roast. Halfway through the roasting process, turn the roast in the cooking liquid.

Once the roast is fully cooked, remove it from the pan and set aside in a large, heatproof pan or dish. Place the braising pan back on the stovetop over high heat and cook until the sauce has reduced down to your desired consistency. Strain the sauce over the cooked roast, discarding the solids.

At this point the roast can either be served or stored in the refrigerator, covered, for up to five days. When ready to serve, reheat the roast in its liquid in a preheated 375°F oven until hot all of the way through.

TO MAKE THE FLAGEOLET: Preheat the oven to 350°F.

Place the beans in a bowl and cover with water. Cover the bowl with plastic wrap and refrigerate overnight. The next day, drain the beans and rinse well with water.

Place an ovenproof braising pan on the stovetop over medium heat and add the oil. When hot, add the onions, celery, carrots, and garlic. Cook until the vegetables have softened and are lightly browned.

Add the soaked beans to the pot and then stir in the broth, bay leaf, and rosemary. Add enough additional water to the pot to cover the beans and bring everything to a simmer. Cover the pot and place in the oven for 40 minutes. Remove the lid, season with salt and pepper, and return the pot, covered, to the oven for an additional 30 minutes. The beans should be tender with just a little bit of water remaining on the bottom of the dish. The beans can be made in advance, cooled and then stored, covered, in the refrigerator until ready to use. To reheat, add a little water or stock to the pan and place in a preheated 375°F oven until the beans are warmed all of the way through.

TO MAKE THE GARNISH: Place the figs and apricots into a dish and then cover them with boiling water until they are fully rehydrated. This will take about 30 minutes. The figs and apricots will be the garnish for the lamb.

Serve this dish family style with the beans underneath the sliced lamb roast and the fruit and mint sprinkled over the meat.

CROWN RACK OF LAMB WITH SPRING-VEGETABLE BAYALDI

SERVES 6

Despite the grandeur of its presentation, a spectacular-looking crown roast is like any other roast – you just stick it in the oven. Moreover, it's as easy as a boned one to carve. A crown is made from two or more loin roasts, from the choice muscle that's tucked alongside the backbone and back ribs. The backbone is sawed off to make the roasts flexible enough to curve and tie together – a task that your butcher (meaning our butcher) will do for you. To serve the crown, you just cut between the ribs.

Two lamb rib racks, joined, are enough for four to six people. Racks vary in size, so order by weight.

Roast:

2 lamb rib racks (approximately 1¼ pounds each), tied

3 tablespoons extra virgin olive oil

2 teaspoons ground cumin

Salt and white pepper

Spring-vegetable bayaldi:

4 tablespoons extra virgin olive oil

2 medium-sized Spanish onions, peeled and thinly sliced

1 medium-sized fennel, bulb only, cleaned and thinly sliced

6 cloves garlic, peeled and thinly sliced

1 medium-sized eggplant, skin on, cut crosswise into ¼-inch rounds

1 medium-sized zucchini, skin on, cut crosswise into ¼-inch rounds

1 medium-sized yellow squash, skin on, cut crosswise into ¼-inch rounds

4 medium-sized fresh plum tomatoes, cored and cut lengthwise into ¼-inch slices

Salt and white pepper

1 bunch thyme, leaves only

TO COOK THE LAMB: Preheat the oven to 450°F.

Place the lamb roast in a 17-inch roasting pan. Drizzle the lamb with oil and season with cumin, salt and pepper.

Place the lamb in the oven and roast for about 25 minutes, or until the internal temperature reaches 125°F, which will yield a medium-rare center.

When the lamb is cooked to your liking, remove it from the pan and let it rest for 15 minutes before slicing.

While the lamb is cooling, make the vegetables.

TO MAKE THE VEGETABLES: Preheat the oven to 350°F.

Place an 8-inch sauté pan on the stovetop over me-

dium heat and add the oil. When the pan is hot, add the onions, fennel, and garlic and cook until they are well caramelized.

Layer the sautéed vegetables along the bottom of an 8 by 8-inch casserole dish.

Season the vegetables slices with salt and pepper and sprinkle evenly with thyme leaves.

Alternating vegetables, layer the seasoned vegetables into the casserole dish, placing them as closely together as possible.

Cover the dish with aluminum foil, place in the oven, and bake until the eggplant and squash are cooked all the way through and soft to the touch, which may take anywhere from 30 to 40 minutes.

When ready to serve, remove the butcher twine from the roast and cut the lamb into chops by slicing in between the bones. Spoon out a portion of the vegetable bayaldi onto each plate and add two or three lamb chops per person.

RACK OF LAMB WITH HERB CRUST

SERVES 6

I can't think of another cut of meat that bespeaks dining elegance quite like a lamb rack. When choosing a rack, you want a nice big eye and good marbling. The extra fat will help to keep the meat tender during cooking. The American racks are far superior to the less expensive Australian or New Zealand racks. For one thing, they are larger. The other two feed their lambs on an exclusively grass diet, while the American lambs are fed grass and then finish their feeding with grains. The grains help to fatten up the lambs and take away from the gamey flavors that are sometimes associated with lamb.

Crumb coating:

2 cups finely ground fresh breadcrumbs

3 tablespoons finely chopped
fresh flat-leaf (Italian) parsley

1 tablespoon finely chopped fresh mint

1½ teaspoon freshly minced rosemary

2 tablespoons extra virgin olive oil

Salt and freshly ground black pepper

Lamb:

2 tablespoons extra virgin olive oil

Salt and freshly ground black pepper

3 (1½-pound) Frenched racks of lamb
(about 8 ribs each), trimmed of all but
a thin layer of fat, room temperature

3 tablespoons Dijon mustard

[SIDENOTE: Procuring the best ingredients is always the most important step in any recipe. Find a good butcher (hmmm, I believe Le Marais has one) and have him choose three nice fresh racks and trim them properly for you. The heavy layers of fat should be removed, yet a thin layer of fat should remain on the lamb to help protect the meat while it is being seared. All the bones should be Frenched as well. This means that the bone should be clean of any meat or fat before cooking.]

TO MAKE THE CRUMB COATING: Place the breadcrumbs, parsley, mint, and rosemary in a bowl and mix well with a spoon. Drizzle in the olive oil, season with salt and pepper, and mix well to combine.

[SIDENOTE: You can also mix this in the bowl of a food processor fitted with the blade attachment. Using a food processor will give the crumb coating a distinctive green color, which I prefer. Up to you, of course.]

TO MAKE THE LAMB: Preheat the oven to 425°F.

Place an 8-inch sauté pan on the stovetop over medium heat and add the oil. Generously season the lamb with salt and pepper. When the pan is hot, add the lamb, fat side down, and sear until you get a deep brown color. Use a pair of tongs to flip over the rack and cook until seared on all sides. Searing is an important part of the flavor development, so don't be impatient. When done, remove each piece and set aside until all of the meat has been seared.

Schmear the mustard all over the eye of the lamb racks. Be sure to cover all of the meat. Evenly divide the crumb coating into three portions. Spread the coating over the mustard, gently patting down the crumbs so that they adhere to the mustard.

Place the racks on a parchment paper-covered baking sheet and roast in the oven for about 15 minutes, or until the internal temperature of the lamb reaches 130°F for medium-rare lamb. Remove the lamb from the oven and allow the rack to rest on a cutting board for 15 minutes before serving.

{SIDENOTE: To get the truest temperature of the cooked meat, place the meat thermometer in the center of the eye.]

TO SERVE: Impress your guests by presenting the whole lamb racks at the table. Then use your sharpest knife to lop off beautiful double lamb chops and leave you guests talking behind your back about how much they hate you for being such a show off.

Veal

Unless you are a vegan, there just isn't any reasonable argument against the consumption of veal. You'll eat a steer as long as we check its ID and it's of age? Save your phony humanitarianism; I'm not interested in your hypocrisy. Besides, veal is delicious, tender, and relatively low in saturated fat in comparison to beef.

Veal Scaloppini

Serves 6

Veal scaloppini is so often overlooked. What I love about a scaloppini of any kind is that it's a quick cook for a weeknight as well as an elegant option for dinner guests.

3 tablespoons extra virgin olive oil

1 cup instant or all-purpose flour

Salt and white pepper

6 (5-ounce) veal scaloppini

4 tablespoons (½ stick / ¼ cup) unsalted margarine

2 tablespoons red wine vinegar

2 tablespoons drained small capers

3 tablespoons fresh flat leaf (Italian) parsley, coarsely chopped

3 cups loosely packed baby arugula, rinsed

1½ cups cherry tomatoes, rinsed, stemmed and halved

Juice of 2 lemons

2 small shallots, peeled and thinly sliced

Place an 8-inch skillet on the stovetop over medium-high heat and add the oil. Place the flour on a plate and season with salt and pepper. Piece by piece dredge the veal in the flour to fully coat all sides, knocking off any excess flour. Once the oil beings to lightly smoke, add half of the scaloppini to the pan. Cook for about two minutes per side to brown, flipping each piece over when browned. Remove the veal from the pan and repeat with the remaining scaloppini.

Wipe out as much oil from the pan as possible and add the margarine, vinegar, and capers. Swirl around, or stir together, to form a sauce. Return the scaloppini to the pan and coat in the sauce.

Place the arugula, tomatoes, and shallots in a large bowl and toss with the lemon juice and a splash of olive oil. Season the salad with salt and pepper.

Place one scaloppini in the center of each plate. Top with a mound of salad and serve.

VEAL VIENNOISE

SERVES 8

I certainly have in the past not shown any great affinity for my cigarette-sucking friends from across the Atlantic, but I have to give credit where it is due. They do have a way with words. For example the veal cutlet, which sounds so pedestrian, is known as Veau Viennoise. If you can swing the expense, instead of using the shoulder cut that is called for in the recipe, have your butcher pound out a bone in veal chop.

Garnish:

2 large eggs, hard-boiled and peeled (see page 62)

3 tablespoons capers, rinsed and drained

2 lemons, peeled and cut into ¼-inch rounds

4 tablespoons fresh flat leaf (Italian) parsley

4 tablespoons chopped Spanish onion

Veal:

4 large eggs

½ cup instant or all-purpose flour

Salt and freshly ground black pepper

3 cups Japanese-style bread crumbs

8 (5-ounce) veal scaloppini, lean shoulder cuts

2 cups extra virgin olive oil

TO MAKE THE GARNISH: Separate the hard-boiled yolks from the whites. If you have a micro-plane zester, grate the white and then yolks. Otherwise, just chop them each up finely and set aside separately.

Mix together the lemons, capers, onions, and parsley and reserve on the side.

TO MAKE THE VEAL: Place the eggs in a large bowl along with 4 tablespoons of water and whisk to combine. Season with salt and pepper.

Place the flour in a large bowl. Season with salt and pepper and mix to combine.

Place the bread crumbs in a large bowl. Season with salt and pepper and mix to combine.

Season the veal with salt and pepper. Working piece by piece, first dredge the veal in the flour to fully coat all sides, knocking off any excess flour. Next, dip each piece into the egg wash, holding them over the bowl to allow any excess batter to drip off. Lastly, dredge the scaloppini in the bread crumbs, making sure that all sides of the meat are fully covered. Place the floured, battered, and breaded scaloppini on a clean plate and repeat until all of the scaloppini are ready to be cooked.

Place a 10-inch, straight-sided sauté pan on the stovetop over medium heat and add the oil. When the oil is hot, add the scaloppini to the pan and cook until golden brown on all sides. Watch the heat, don't let the oil get too hot or it will burn the crumb coating. The scaloppini should only take about two minutes per side to cook if the heat is right. You may need to cook the veal in batches to avoid overcrowding the pan. When ready, remove the veal from the pan and drain on paper towel.

Serve the veal on a platter, generously topped with the prepared garnish.

PAN-ROASTED VEAL MEDALLIONS WITH ROASTED TOMATOES, ROSEMARY, AND FENNEL

SERVES 6

In and of itself, veal is for the most part a textural experience. The nature of veal is that it has very little flavor on its own. This will bring some wonderful fresh flavors to what is essentially bland meat. Cook to medium at most, otherwise it will be tough and virtually inedible.

12 (3-ounce) veal loin medallions

Salt and freshly ground black pepper

4 tablespoons extra virgin olive oil, divided

2 cups dry white wine, such as chardonnay

6 sprigs rosemary

4 tablespoons (½ stick / ¾ cup) unsalted margarine

2 pints cherry tomatoes, rinsed, stemmed, and halved

1 medium-sized fennel, bulb only, cleaned and thinly sliced

1 large Spanish onion, peeled and thinly sliced

3 cloves garlic, peeled and sliced

Preheat the oven to 400°F.

Season both sides of the veal loins generously with salt and pepper.

Place an 8-inch skillet on the stovetop over high heat and add the oil. Add the veal medallions to the pan and sear, or brown, on all sides. This should take not more than four minutes per side. When seared, place the medallions on a clean baking sheet. You may need to sear the meat in batches to avoid overcrowding the pan. Once all of the veal has been seared, place the baking sheet in the oven and cook the veal for about four minutes for a medium-rare center. Remove the medallions from the oven and allow them to rest for about eight minutes before serving.

Add the wine to the same skillet as the rendered fat and deglaze the pan, making sure to scrape the browned bits off bottom of the pan. Bring the wine to a boil, add 2 sprigs of the rosemary and the margarine and reduce the sauce to a consistency thick enough to coat the back of a spoon. Season with salt and pepper.

Place the tomatoes, fennel, onion, garlic, and the remaining 4 sprigs of rosemary on a clean baking sheet. Drizzle with oil and season with salt and pepper. Roast the vegetables in the oven for 12 minutes. When ready, the fennel and onions should be browned and the tomatoes caramelized and softened. Pour the contents of the tray, including all of the liquid into a clean container and keep warm until ready to serve.

To serve, spoon the sauce over the medallions and garnish the meat with the roasted tomato mixture.

BRAISED VEAL TONGUE

SERVES 8

I feel the need to come clean on this dish. I don't like tongue. If I didn't make myself clear, I hate tongue. As a matter of fact, the only time that you will ever find tongue available at Le Marais is when the chef (me) is on vacation. Jose takes that three-week period to do all of the stuff that I refuse to do during the other 49 weeks of the year. However, keep in mind that I am a professional and every day I cook things that I haven't any interest in eating at that moment. The boss likes this; hopefully you will too.

3 tablespoons extra virgin olive oil

2 medium-sized Spanish onions, peeled and cut into ¼-inch dice

3 ribs celery, cut into ¼-inch dice

1 medium-sized carrot, peeled and cut into ¼-inch dice

2 whole veal tongues, about 3 pounds total

6 quarts veal stock (page 2)

1 head garlic, cloves only

1½ cups white wine

1 jalapeño

Salt and freshly ground black pepper

Preheat the oven to 325°F.

Place an 8-inch skillet on the stovetop over high heat and add the oil. When the pan is hot, add the onions, celery, and carrot and cook until softened and browned, about eight to nine minutes.

Place the veal tongues, sautéed vegetables, veal stock, garlic, white wine, and jalapeño in a 9 x 13-inch roasting pan. Cover the pan tightly with foil and roast in the oven for 3½ hours. The tongues are finished when you can insert and remove a paring knife into the thickest part of the tongue with no resistance at all. Remove the tongues from the pan and set aside to cool.

Place the roasting pan with all the juices on the stovetop over medium heat and cook until the roasting liquid has reduced down to 1½ cups. Strain the liquid into a clean bowl, discarding the solids. Season the broth with salt and pepper.

When the tongues have cooled enough to touch, peel off the skin. To do this, use the tip of your knife on the underside of the tongue to slice the tongue down the center, slicing just deep enough to loosen some of the skin to grab hold of with your hands. Use a clean cloth to grab the skin and pull it back away from the flesh. If the skin is difficult to remove, the tongue isn't cold enough.

Cutting with the grain, cut the tongue into ½-inch-thick slices. Divide the slices among plates and sauce with the reduced broth. Serve with a side of potato purée or with a fresh parsley and shallot salad.

PAN-ROASTED VEAL CHOP WITH SHERRY GREEN PEPPERCORN SAUCE

SERVES 6

The veal chop is a steakhouse classic. It's simple to make and impressive as hell for your guests.

6 (1½-inch-thick) veal chops, bone-in

Salt and white pepper

4 tablespoons extra virgin olive oil

2 cloves garlic, peeled and thinly sliced

1 small bunch thyme

3 tablespoons (approximately ⅓ stick) unsalted margarine

1 large shallot, peeled and cut into ¼-inch dice

4 tablespoons sherry

3 tablespoons brined green peppercorns, rinsed and drained

2 cups veal stock (page 2)

3 tablespoons freshly chopped flat leaf (Italian) parsley

Rind of 1 lemon

Preheat the oven to 375°F.

Place the veal chops in a shallow dish. Season the chops with salt and pepper and rub both sides with the garlic slices and thyme. Set aside covered, at room temperature and marinate for three hours.

Place a 10-inch skillet on the stovetop over high heat and add the oil. Use paper towel to wipe off and discard as much of the marinade from veal chops as you can, and add the chops to the pan. Sear, or brown, the chops until very well browned, about four minutes on each side. Remove the chops from the pan and place on a clean baking sheet. You may need to cook the chops in batches to avoid overcrowding the pan. When all of the chops have been seared, place the baking sheet in the oven and roast the veal for seven minutes for a medium-rare center. Remove the chops from the oven and allow them to rest for about eight minutes before serving.

Add the margarine and shallots to the same skillet with the rendered fat and cook for two minutes until tender and slightly browned. Add the sherry to the pan and cook until the sherry has reduced down to about one tablespoon. Add the veal stock, lemon rind, and peppercorns, bring to a boil and reduce the sauce down to about 1½ cups. Season with salt and pepper, and stir in the parsley.

Serve the chops with the sherry peppercorn sauce on top or on the side.

MARINATED RACK OF VEAL WITH SALSIFY AND CHIMICHURRI SAUCE

SERVES 8

The chimichurri sauce is a fantastic all-purpose sauce that works with every protein that I can think off. Perfect in the summer for a BBQ as well as on a braise in the winter. It brings fresh, bright flavors to everything.

Marinade:
Zest of 2 lemons

3 cloves garlic

1 tablespoon fennel seed

1 small bunch basil, leaves only

White pepper

4 tablespoons extra virgin olive oil

1 (4½-pound) veal rack, frenched

3 tablespoons extra virgin olive oil

Salsify:
1½ pounds salsify (about 12 pieces)

2 lemons, halved

2 tablespoons extra virgin olive oil

2 tablespoons freshly chopped flat leaf (Italian) parsley

Chimichurri sauce:
1 bunch mint

1 bunch flat leaf (Italian) parsley

1 bunch fresh basil

6 cloves garlic, peeled

½ cup red wine vinegar

1½ cups extra virgin olive oil

3 tablespoons granulated sugar

Salt and white pepper

TO MAKE THE VEAL: Place the lemon zest, garlic, fennel seed, basil leaves, pepper, and oil in the bowl of a food processor fitted with the blade attachment and process to a paste. Completely coat the veal rack with the paste. Place the rack on a plate, cover with plastic wrap and chill in the refrigerator for about six hours or overnight.

When ready to cook the veal, use paper towel wipe off and discard as much of the marinade from the veal as you can, then season the veal with salt.

Preheat the oven to 375°F.

Place a 10-inch skillet on the stovetop over medium-high heat and add the oil. Add the veal to the pan and sear, or brown, on all sides until well browned.

Place the veal rack on a clean baking sheet and roast in the oven until the center of the veal reaches an internal temperature of 145°F. Remove the veal from the oven and allow the roast the rest for at least 15 minutes before you cut into it.

TO MAKE THE SALSIFY: Fill a large bowl with cold water and set aside.

Use a vegetable peeler to peel the black bark from the salsify. Hold them in the cold water until ready to cook or for up to 30 minutes, to keep the salsify from oxidizing, or turning brown.

When all of the salsify has been peeled, place a 4-quart stockpot on the stovetop over medium-high heat and fill half full with water. Generously salt the water and bring to a boil. Add the salsify and the lemon halves and cook until the salsify is fork tender. Remove the salsify from the water, drizzle with a little extra virgin olive oil, and sprinkle with chopped parsley.

If you are not using the salsify immediately, submerge in a bowl of ice water to stop the cooking. When cool to the touch, drain the water and pat the salsify dry. Reserve the salsify in the refrigerator until ready to use, or for up to two days. Gently reheat the salsify on the stovetop in an 8-inch pan with a little extra virgin olive oil, and sprinkle with parsley before serving.

TO MAKE THE CHIMICHURRI SAUCE: Place all of the ingredients in the bowl of a food processor fitted with the blade attachment and pulse until well combined. This is best when made just before serving; it doesn't hold well and the sauce tends to oxidize after a few hours.

Osso Bucco

Serves 8

5 tablespoons extra virgin olive oil

8 veal shanks (about 6 pounds), cross cut and tied with kitchen twine

Salt and freshly ground black pepper

½ cup instant or all-purpose flour

3 tablespoons (approximately ⅓ stick) unsalted margarine

2 medium-sized Spanish onions, peeled and cut into ¼-inch dice

1 medium-sized carrot, peeled and cut into ¼-inch dice

1 rib celery, cut into ¼-inch dice

3 cloves garlic, peeled and thinly sliced

2 cup dry white wine, such as chardonnay

2 cups chicken stock (page 3)

1 (28-ounce) can whole plum tomatoes, juices reserved, cut into ¼-inch dice

1 cup pitted black olives, halved

8 sprigs thyme

3 sprigs flat leaf (Italian) parsley

2 fresh bay leaves

Zest of 1 lemon, cut into thick slices

Gremolata garnish:

1 tablespoon finely zested lemon zest

1½ tablespoons fresh thyme, leaves only, coarsely chopped

3 tablespoons finely chopped fresh flat leaf (Italian) parsley, leaves only

Preheat the oven to 325°F.

Place a heavy-bottomed, 6-quart, lidded Dutch oven on the stovetop over medium-high heat and add the oil. Season the veal shanks very liberally with salt and pepper.

Place the flour on a plate or in a bowl. Thoroughly dredge the shanks in the flour until completely coated, knocking off any excess flour. Add the shanks to the hot pan and sear, or brown on all sides. Good rich coloring is vital for the flavor of the meat and the sauce, so let the meat be and allow the shanks to brown very well. You may need to sear the meat in batches to avoid overcrowding the pan. When all of the meat has been seared, set aside until ready to use.

Once all of the meat has been seared, add the margarine to the same pan as the rendered fat. When melted, add the onion, carrot, and celery and cook until softened and well browned, about eight minutes. Stir in the garlic and cook for an additional two minutes. Add the chicken stock, white wine, diced tomatoes, olives, fresh herbs, and lemon zest, and season with salt and pepper. Return the veal shanks to the pan and bring everything to a boil. Cover the pot with a lid and cook in the oven for 2½ hours, until the meat is fork tender.

TO MAKE THE GREMOLATA: Place all of the ingredients in a small bowl and mix until combined.

I like to serve the Osso Bucco with a starchy side dish like creamy polenta, pommes purée or egg noodles. Place the starch of your choice in the center of each plate or bowl and top with the Osso Bucco. Cover with the vegetables and braising liquid and top with gremolata.

Rolled Veal-Breast Roast with Garlic, Thyme, and Pine Nuts

Serves 8

We can all agree that cooking kosher definitely has its limitations. When people are coming over, I'm always searching for something a little different to serve. The beauty of this roast is that because of the fat content, it is difficult to overcook and dry out.

Stuffing:

2 cups currants

1 cup brandy

2 cups fresh bread crumbs, cut into 1-inch dice

5 cloves garlic, peeled and thinly sliced

1 small bunch thyme, leaves only

1 cup pine nuts, roasted and cooled

2 small shallots, peeled and thinly sliced

Veal:

1 (4-pound) veal breast, trimmed

Salt and freshly ground black pepper

4 tablespoons extra virgin olive oil

1 cup dry white wine, such as pinot gris

1 cup chicken stock (page 3)

Salt and freshly ground black pepper

TO MAKE THE STUFFING: Place the currants in a small, heatproof bowl.

Place a 2-quart saucepan on the stovetop over medium heat, add the brandy and bring to a boil. Pour the brandy over the currants and allow them to soak for at least 30 minutes.

Remove the currants from the soaking liquid and then place them, along with the bread crumbs, garlic, thyme, pine nuts, and shallots in a large bowl and mix to combine. Season with salt and pepper.

TO MAKE THE VEAL: Preheat the oven to 300°F. Lay the veal flat on a clean work surface and spread the breast apart. Season the inside with salt and pepper. Use a spoon or spatula to spread the stuffing evenly over the inside of the breast. Roll the breast up lengthwise, rolling as tight as you can. Use kitchen twine to tie the breast together snugly, tying every 2-inches down the length of the roll. Season the outside of the roast liberally with salt and pepper.

Place a 9 by 13-inch roasting pan on the stovetop over high heat and add the oil. When the pan is hot and the oil begins to smoke, add the roast. Sear, or brown, the roast very, very well on all sides; each side should be a rich brown color. Remove the roast from the pan and add the wine to deglaze the pan, making sure to scrape all of the bits and pieces from the bottom of the pan. Add the chicken stock, bring everything to a boil and return the seared roast to the pan.

Place the meat in the oven and roast for about two hours. After the first 90 minutes, insert a food thermometer into the center of the roast to check the internal temperature. The roast is ready when the thermometer reads 160°F.

When ready, remove the roast from the oven and let it rest for 20 minutes before you slice into it.

Poultry

In my humble opinion, there is no other protein on the planet that is so simple in preparation, yet so complex in flavor and textures, than that of the whole roasted chicken. In my 20 years in the professional kitchen, there is little that I take so much pleasure in than running a baguette through the bottom of a pan of roasted chickens and mopping up the salty, fatty, sweet juices on the bottom.

Airline Breast of Chicken Forestiere

Serves 6

The airline breast is a more sophisticated way of serving the usually boring chicken breast. Also, cooking it in this fashion helps to keep the meat from drying out.

Chicken breasts:

Extra virgin olive oil

6 fresh chicken breasts with wings attached, skin on

Salt and white pepper

3 cups dry white wine, such as chardonnay

1 small bunch thyme

4 tablespoons (½ stick / ¼ cup) unsalted margarine

Sauce Forestiere:

5 tablespoons (approximately ⅔ stick / ⅓ cup) unsalted margarine

2 small shallots, peeled and minced

2 cloves garlic, peeled and sliced

1 small bunch thyme

1½ pounds wild mushrooms

1½ cups veal stock (page 2)

TO MAKE THE CHICKEN BREASTS: Preheat the oven to 400°F. Place a non-stick, 10-inch skillet on the stovetop over medium-high heat and add oil. Season both sides of the chicken breasts liberally with salt and pepper. When the pan is hot, sear, or brown, the chicken pieces skin side down. Sear until the skin becomes very well browned and crisp, about six to nine minutes. You may need to sear the chicken in batches to avoid overcrowding the pan. Once all of the chicken has been seared, place the pieces meat side down on a clean baking sheet and set aside. You are searing only the skin side for texture; searing the meat side will dry out the meat.

Add the wine, thyme, and margarine to the same pan with the rendered fat, and cook until the liquid has reduced by half.

Place the baking sheet with the chicken in the oven and carefully pour the reduced cooking liquid into the bottom of the pan. Roast for nine minutes until the chicken is firm to the touch yet still has a little resistance to it when poked with your finger.

TO MAKE THE SAUCE: Place a 10-inch skillet on the stovetop over medium heat and add the margarine, shallots, garlic, and thyme. Cook gently until softened and slightly browned. Add the mushrooms and the veal stock and cook until the mushrooms are tender and the sauce has reduced and thickened enough to glaze the mushrooms; this will take about 13 to 15 minutes.

TO FINISH THE DISH: When the chicken is ready, remove the pan from the oven and place the chicken pieces on a cutting board. Pour the remaining cooking liquid from the baking sheet into the mushroom sauce and stir well to combine. Season the sauce with salt and pepper.

To serve, cut each breast into five slices and fan them onto a plate, being sure to serve the wing piece as well. Generously cover with mushroom sauce. I like this dish served with Israeli couscous or pommes purée.

DEEP-FRIED CHICKEN

SERVES 8

I can't think of any dish that creates the frenzy in the Le Marais kitchen the way that fried chicken does. We don't sell it on the menu or tableside at the restaurant solely because it just doesn't fit with what we do here. We do, however, sell it on occasion to our catering customers. When the order sheet hits the kitchen the day before, we all prepare to stuff ourselves with a fried-chicken lunch the next day.

6 cups unflavored, nondairy coffee creamer

Juice of 4 lemons

Salt and white pepper

1 teaspoon Old Bay Seasoning

½ teaspoon chili powder

½ teaspoon powdered mustard

½ teaspoon red pepper flakes

1 bunch thyme, leaves only

2 cloves garlic, peeled

2 fresh whole chickens, cut into 10 pieces each as follows: 2 legs, 2 thighs, 2 wings, 2 breasts each cut in half

1 gallon peanut oil or as needed

6 cups all-purpose flour

10 large eggs

2 cups water

Day 1/Step 1

Place the creamer, lemon juice, salt, white pepper, Old Bay Seasoning, chili powder, powdered mustard, pepper flakes, and thyme in a large bowl and mix to combine. Use a micro-plane zester to grate the garlic cloves into the mixture. Place the chicken in the marinade, making sure that all of the pieces are submerged. Cover the bowl with plastic wrap and place in the refrigerator overnight to marinate.

Day 2/Step 2

Remove the chicken from the marinade.

Place a heavy-bottomed, 8-quart stockpot on the stovetop over medium heat and fill it half full with peanut oil. Insert a candy thermometer and heat the oil to 350°F. Then lower the temperature on the stovetop to low heat, being careful to maintain the temperature of the oil at 350°F and not allowing it to go higher. If the oil gets too hot, the exterior of the chicken will cook too quickly and toughen the crust.

While the oil is heating, prepare the chicken. Place the flour in a large bowl and season with salt and pepper. Place the eggs and water in a separate bowl, season with salt and pepper, and whisk well to combine.

Working in batches, dredge the chicken in the flour. Remove the chicken from the flour and knock off any excess flour. Gently drop the well-floured chicken pieces into the egg batter and thoroughly coat. Remove the chicken pieces from the egg and shake gently to allow any excess batter to drain off. Return the chicken to the flour for a second coating, knocking off the excess flour upon removal.

Still working in batches, gently place the chicken in the hot oil and fry until the chicken is crisp and very well browned. Keep in mind that the dark meat will take longer to cook than the white meat. Give the dark meat about 13 to 14 minutes per piece, while the white meat should only take eight to 10 minutes. Keep an eye on the oil and adjust the temperature on the stovetop as needed to keep the oil from cooling down or becoming too hot.

When the chicken is ready, remove each piece from the hot oil and drain on a paper towel. Serve while still hot. The fried chicken can be stored in the refrigerator for up to four or five days. I like to eat it cold; I find that reheating it just isn't up to snuff.

POULET GRAND-MÈRE

SERVES 8

I use this as a version of coq au vin at the restaurant. The truly classic version of this dish uses red wine. However, I recently made an adjustment to the recipe that has been very popular in the restaurant. I replaced the red wine with white and added the no-brainer element of bacon to it (Le Marais bacon, not that heinous beef-fry garbage that is often used as a bacon substitute in kosher kitchens). The standard coq au vin is in the book as well. I recommend that you take your time and enjoy the process. Like all home cooking, it's best done with a glass of wine by your side.

¼ cup extra virgin olive oil

2 fresh whole chickens, cut into 8 pieces each

Salt and freshly ground black pepper

2 medium-sized Spanish onions, peeled and cut into ½-inch dice

2 ribs celery, cut into ½-inch lengths

1½ medium-sized carrots, peeled and cut into ½-inch lengths

6 cloves garlic, peeled and sliced

1 tablespoons tomato paste

2 tablespoons all-purpose flour

2 (750-ml) bottles dry French white wine, such as viognier

½ pound slab veal bacon, cut into ¼-inch-thick slices

1 pound cremini mushrooms

24 red pearl onions, peeled

1½ cups pitted black olives or any other olive that suits you

1 small bunch thyme, 1 fresh bay leaf, 1 tablespoon peppercorns, tied together in a cheesecloth bag.

Place a 6-quart lidded Dutch oven on the stovetop over medium heat and add the oil. Pat the chicken dry with clean paper towel and season with salt and pepper. When the pan is hot, sear, or brown, the chicken pieces skin side down. Once the skin is fully browned, turn over and sear the meat side. If the skin sticks to the bottom of the pan when you try to turn the chicken over, it's not done searing. The idea here is to brown the skin and render out some of the fat from the skin so that later on it will not be rubbery. You may need to work in batches to avoid overcrowding the pan. Once all of the chicken has been seared, set aside until ready to use.

[SIDENOTE: When I say brown, I mean a deep, rich browning. Searing, or browning, is always the most important step of any braised meat dish so now is not the time to get lackadaisical. This is when you develop the color and most importantly the flavors associated with a braised item.]

Add the onions, celery, carrots, and garlic to the same pan with the rendered fat and cook until softened slightly and golden brown, about 10 minutes. Stir in the tomato paste and cook for another four minutes. Sprinkle the flour over the vegetables and mix well with a large spoon so that all of the vegetables are well coated, and cook for another two minutes. Season with salt and pepper. Pour in the white wine and stir until the sauce is smooth.

Are you drinking yet?

Return the chicken to the pan and add the bacon, mushrooms, pearl onions, and the olives. Add enough water to cover the meat and bring everything a boil. Lower the temperature on the stovetop to a slow simmer and add the cheesecloth bag to the pot. Season with salt and pepper, cover the pot with its lid, and simmer for about 1¼ hours. The chicken is cooked through when the juice from the thigh runs clear when pierced and the meat pulls easily away from the bone.

I have a nice little buzz happening. So should you.

Once the chicken is cooked, remove it and the slab of bacon from the stew and set aside. Check the consistency of the sauce; it should be thick enough to heavily coat the back of a spoon. If it is not, strain the sauce through a fine-mesh sieve and into a clean 3-quart saucepan, and set the strained vegetables aside in a bowl to be used for garnish. Place the saucepan on the stovetop over medium-high heat and cook until the sauce has reduced to your desired level of thickness, scraping the bottom of the pan occasionally to prevent any scorching or burning. Season with salt and pepper.

Cut the bacon slabs into ½-inch-thick lardons, or lengths, and mix these in with the reserved vegetables. Serve the chicken over or alongside a starch such as noodles, mashed potatoes, or my favorite, creamy polenta.

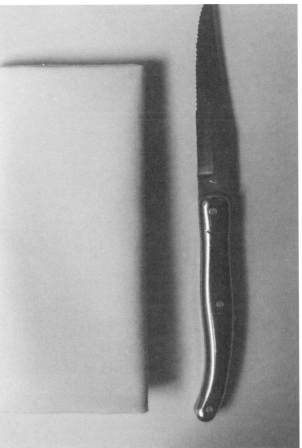

Poulet Roti (Whole Roasted Chicken)

Serves 2, maybe 3, possibly 4

If you've cooked, chances are that you think that you've roasted a chicken. Sure, you put a bird in an oven, you may have even sort of seasoned it, and you may have even stuffed the cavity while making some sort of off-color joke about it. That doesn't mean that you properly roasted a chicken. Most chicken that I have tasted was either dry, undercooked, or the biggest sin of all, had limp rubbery skin.

Chicken should taste like chicken. Keep it simple. Make a simple pan sauce at the end, as I will explain, and this will be a staple in your arsenal.

1 (3½-pound) fresh whole chicken

Salt and white pepper

1 lemon

4 cloves garlic, peeled, divided

1 medium-sized Spanish onion, peeled and cut into ½-inch dice, divided

1 bunch thyme, divided

1 (750-ml) bottle white wine, such as chardonnay

2 tablespoons extra virgin olive oil

Freshly ground black pepper

1 bunch flat leaf (Italian) parsley, coarsely chopped

Preheat the oven to 350°F.

Remove the packet of giblets from the center of the bird, if it has one, and reserve. Thoroughly rinse the chicken inside and out with cold water. Pat the chicken dry with a clean paper towel and place it on a cutting board breast side up.

Season the inside of the cavity with salt and white pepper. Cut the lemon in half and place the first half inside the cavity of the chicken, placing it all the way in. Follow with two garlic cloves, half of the onion, and half of the thyme

Truss the bird by crossing the legs and pushing them up into the sides of the breasts. Then loop butcher's twine numerous times around the crossed legs as

tightly as possible. Tie the twine good and tight and cut off the excess. Tuck the tips of the wings underneath the breasts. This is a simple and yet very effective method of trussing a bird. Trussing is an important step as it allows the chicken to cook more evenly.

Add the remaining 2 cloves garlic, the other half of the onion, the reserved giblets, and 1 cup of the wine to the bottom of a 12 by 17-inch roasting pan.

Drizzle the oil liberally over the top of the chicken and use your hands to rub it all over the skin. Season the chicken well with salt and black pepper. Place the seasoned chicken on top of the onions and giblets.

Place the pan in the oven and roast the chicken for 30 minutes, basting occasionally with the wine and rendered fat on the bottom of the pan. Since most ovens have hot spots, rotate the pan at least once to ensure the chicken cooks and browns evenly.

After 30 minutes, jack up the oven temperature up to 450°F. Roast the whole chicken for another 30 minutes. Don't forget to baste.

To check for doneness, insert a skewer into the joint between the leg and the thigh. If the juices run clear, you're good to go. Remove the chicken from the pan and place it onto your serving platter to rest for about 15 minutes before carving.

Place the roasting pan on the stovetop over high heat. Stir in the remaining wine and thyme and scrape the bottom of the pan with a wooden spoon to get up the fond. Bring the wine to a boil and cook until the sauce has reduced by half. Strain the sauce into a clean container, discarding the solids. Season with salt and pepper, and garnish with chopped parsley before serving.

ROAST TURKEY WITH SAGE AND WHITE-WINE GRAVY

SERVES 10

The carving of turkey, or a chicken for that matter, needs to done on a carving board, not in a dining-room table in front of the awful, judgmental eyes of your family, all of whom are secretly awaiting your destruction of the holiday centerpiece. Present the whole roasted bird to the animals first, and then return it to the kitchen for the proper breaking down. Follow the same procedure for any whole roasted bird.

---

1 (10-pound) fresh whole turkey

1 small Spanish onion, peeled and cut into a ½-inch dice

1 medium-sized carrot, peeled and cut into a ½-inch dice

1 rib celery, cut into a ½-inch dice

1 quart chicken stock (page 3)

½ cup extra virgin olive oil, divided

Salt and white pepper

4 sprigs sage

1 lemon, halved

2 large carrots, halved lengthwise

4 celery stalks, halved lengthwise

5 tablespoons (approximately ⅔ stick / ⅓ cup) unsalted margarine

⅓ cup all-purpose flour

1 cup dry white wine, such as chardonnay

Preheat the oven to 425°F.

Remove the neck and the giblets from the cavity of the turkey.

Place a 3-quart saucepan on the stovetop over high heat. Add the neck, giblets, onion, carrot, diced celery, and chicken stock and bring to a boil. Lower the temperature on the stovetop to low and simmer until the liquid has reduced to about 2 cups. Strain the stock through a fine-mesh sieve and into a clean bowl and set aside to be used to make the gravy.

Rinse the turkey inside and out with cold water and pat dry. Coat the turkey inside and out with half of the olive oil. Season the outside of the turkey liberally with the salt and pepper, patting it into the skin to adhere. Place the sage and lemon inside the cavity of the turkey.

If you are using a roasting pan with a rack, place the turkey on the rack inside a 12 by 17-inch roasting pan. If the roasting pan doesn't have a rack, arrange the halved carrots and celery stalks along the bottom of the roasting pan. Place the turkey on top of the carrots and celery so that the turkey does not rest directly on the bottom of the pan. Drizzle the turkey with the remaining ¼ cup of olive oil.

Place the turkey in the oven and roast until an instant read thermometer inserted deep into the thigh, but away from the bone, reads 160°F, and the juices in the thigh run clear when pierced. While this should take about 2 to 2½ hours, begin checking after two hours. When the turkey is fully cooked, remove it from the pan and let rest for 15 minutes before carving. The pan juices will be used for the gravy.

While the turkey is resting, make the gravy. Place a heavy-bottomed, 2-quart saucepan on the stovetop over medium heat and add the margarine. Once the margarine has melted, whisk in the flour and cook, whisking, for three to four minutes, to make a blond roux. The roux will act as a thickening agent in the gravy. Whisk in the white wine and cook, whisking, until the mixture begins to thicken. Pour in the pan juices and the reserved turkey stock, and raise the temperature on the stovetop to high heat. Stir to combine and bring everything to a boil. Then lower the temperature on the stovetop to low heat and let the sauce simmer until thickened and ready to serve. To remove any lumps that may have formed while making the gravy, simply strain through a fine-mesh sieve and into a clean serving container.

You will need to have a sharp carving knife and a good strong carving fork.

Start with the legs. Cut through the skin at the juncture where the body/end of the breast cavity meets the thigh and leg. Use the fork to gently pull the leg away from the body while you cut through the joint, slicing right through the joint to remove the leg and the thigh. Repeat with the other leg.

Place the leg skin side down and locate the line at the joint where the thigh and the drumstick meet. Holding your knife along this line, you can slice easily through the joint. If you hit resistance, adjust the angle of the knife and try again. Cut down though the line and separate the thigh from the drumstick. Repeat this process with the other leg.

Remove the wishbone, (also known as the collar-bone) from the turkey. When cooked, it will easily release from the meat. Removing the bone will prevent it from splintering when you carve the meat. Use your fingers to remove the wishbone by simply pulling it out of the front of the bird.

To remove the breast meat, first make sure the turkey is breast side up. Run your knife down the middle of the turkey, through the skin along one side of the breastbone. Then continue to cut down, following the line of the ribs, pulling the meat gently away from the bones in one large piece as you cut, leaving behind as little meat as possible. When you get to the wing joint, cut through it as you did with the thigh joint and continue to remove the breast from the body. Repeat with the other side.

Remove the wings from each breast and cut the breasts crosswise into slices before serving. For even, attractive slices, cut the meat against the grain.

BRAISED DUCK LEGS WITH WHITE PEARL ONIONS AND PETITE POIS

SERVES 4

This braise will transport you to winters in Gascony. Use a bottle of Bordeaux as your red wine for an authentic flavor. Saving an extra bottle for yourself as a beverage goes without saying.

4 fresh duck legs, skin on

Salt and freshly ground black pepper

Vegetable oil

1 small Spanish onion, peeled and cut into ¼-inch dice

2 ribs celery, cut into ¼-inch dice

1 small carrot, cut into ¼-inch dice

2 cloves garlic, peeled and thinly sliced

1 tablespoon tomato paste

2 tablespoons all-purpose flour

1 (750-ml) bottle Bordeaux

1 bunch tarragon

1 cup peeled pearl onions

1 cup frozen baby peas

Preheat the oven to 350°F.

Season the duck legs with salt and pepper. Place a 3-quart, lidded braising pan on the stovetop over medium-high heat and add the oil. When the pan is hot, sear, or brown, the duck pieces skin side down. Once the skin is fully browned, turn the duck over and sear the meat side. If the skin sticks to the bottom of the pan when you try to turn it over, it's not done searing. Once all of the duck has been seared, set aside until ready to use.

Add the onion, celery, carrot, and garlic to the same pan as the rendered fat and cook gently until softened. Stir in the tomato paste and cook for another two minutes. Sprinkle the flour over the vegetables and mix well with a large spoon so that all of the vegetables are well coated. Stir in the wine. Return the duck legs to the pan and then add enough water to just cover the meat. Add the tarragon, and season with salt and pepper. Cover the pan with its

lid and place it in the oven. Cook the duck for two hours, until the meat is tender enough to fall off the bone.

Remove the legs from the pan and place the pan back on the stovetop over high heat. Cook until the sauce has reduced to your desired level of thickness. Strain the sauce through a fine mesh sieve and into a clean bowl, discarding the solids. Season with salt and pepper.

Place a 2-quart saucepot on the stovetop over high heat, fill three-quarters full with water and bring to a boil. Add a generous amount of salt to the water and drop in the pearl onions. Cook until a paring knife can be easily inserted into the center of the onions; this should take about 12 minutes depending upon the size of your onions. Remove the onions from the hot water and immediately submerge them in a bowl of cold water to stop the cooking process. When cold to the touch, drain and set aside.

Place a 2-quart saucepot on the stovetop over high heat, fill three-quarters full with water and bring to a boil. Add a generous amount of salt to the water and drop in the peas. Cook for 60 seconds, just long enough to blanch the peas. Remove the peas from the hot water and immediately submerge them in a bowl of cold water to stop the cooking process. When cold to the touch, drain and set aside.

Serve the hot duck legs over a creamy starch, lightly sauced, and then garnish with the blanched vegetables.

PAN-ROASTED DUCK BREAST WITH PONZU SAUCE AND GRILLED SCALLIONS

SERVES 6

6 pan-roasted duck breasts (page 76)

Sauce:

1 tablespoon corn starch

1 tablespoon cold water

½ cup light soy sauce

¼ cup freshly squeezed orange juice

2 tablespoons freshly
squeezed lemon juice

2 tablespoons freshly squeezed lime juice

1 tablespoon mirin

¼ teaspoon crushed red pepper flakes

Scallions:

12 whole scallions, trimmed

Extra virgin olive oil

Salt and freshly ground black pepper

TO MAKE THE SAUCE: Place the corn starch and the water in a small bowl and whisk to combine.

Place a 2-quart saucepan on the stovetop over medium heat. Add the soy sauce, orange juice, lemon juice, lime juice, mirin, and pepper flakes and stir to combine. Bring the mixture to a simmer and whisk in the corn starch mixture until thickened.

TO GRILL THE SCALLIONS: Place a grill pan on the stovetop over high heat and get it scorching hot. Drizzle the scallions with olive oil and season with salt and pepper. Place the scallions onto the grill pan and char them on all sides.

Cut the prepared duck breasts crosswise into six slices and place in the center of each plate. Spoon some hot sauce over the sliced duck and garnish with the grilled scallions.

Fish

Everybody knows that Le Marais is, and always will be, a steak house. We have lines at the front door for a reason. And that reason is not because I am a bit of a fish Svengali. It's because we take great pains to have aged beef at the ready whenever you come a calling. So neither Jose or I should in any way be delusional enough to believe that I should be able to sell a fair amount of fish specials on any given night. Right? Intellectually, we know better.

However, the heart wants what the heart wants, and damn it, I want to sell more fish. I put a lot of time, effort, and thought into buying top-quality fish from the best purveyors that the world has to offer and all I ask is that just a small percentage of clients order a piece of fish. Too much to ask? Salmon doesn't count!

The big problem is finding that one fish guy who can be counted upon time and time again to give the freshest fish at reasonable prices. This can be difficult. I find that even in a city like New York, finding a fish counter that doesn't sell tired-looking fish is a task and a half. I have been to all of the top markets in the city, and would venture to say that maybe one or two of them doesn't peddle fish that has seen better days. It's a brutal business. They have to buy an expensive product, sell it at a high price, and deal with a product that deteriorates by the minute even in the best of environments. This leaves us in a difficult position, especially since we all know that eating more fish and less meat is recommended by every doctor on the planet. Let me try to walk you through the process that I go through when buying fish for the family.

Firstly, I survey the condition of the store. The nose knows. The smell in the air should be sweet and briny, like the ocean. If it smells at all "fishy" or with an overpowering scent of bleach or cleaning liquids, I turn and walk away. I also take a peek at the cutting areas. Butchers with clean boards have respect for the delicate nature of the fish. Dirty boards = dirty birdies. Pass.

Once past the nose test (which my family loves to tell me that I don't pass every night after work), I take a quick scan of the counter. I want to see the entire thing packed in ice. However, the fish fillets themselves should not be directly on the ice. It's best if they are in a stainless steel tray which is then packed in the ice. Whole fish should be packed thoroughly in ice. I also check for pooling water. If the drainage system in the case isn't working, water pools and leaves behind a pond of stank water, which I don't need my dinner marinating in.

Buying whole fish is the easiest and more trustworthy way of picking out your dinner. The skin should be tight and shiny with firm flesh. The eyes should be clear and bright and not sunken in. The gills should be a bright healthy-looking red color. If it has scales, they should be firmly attached and not easily flaking off. And of course the odor should be sweet and oceany, never fishy or sour smelling.

Buying fresh fish fillets is a more difficult process since there are fewer signs to search for. The fillet should have no discoloration; the color should be bright and shiny. Look for dry spots, ice burns, or signs of water damage. The flesh should be firm all the way around. Smell it. Just like the whole fish, it should smell sweet and briny like the ocean. It's not an easy process, but your health will thank you for the effort.

POACHED COD PROVENÇAL

SERVES 6

The point of this dish is to learn the procedure behind proper fish poaching. I can only hope that I am doing a public service by preventing the unnecessary boiling and desecration of the fish that readily gave its life so that we could enjoy the occasional respite from bull flesh. Same procedure works with halibut, salmon, tuna, or any other fish.

Poaching liquid:

1 cup dry white wine, such as sauvignon blanc or any crisp white wine

2 green tea bags

1 orange, quartered

2 cloves garlic, peeled

5 sprigs thyme

Salt and white pepper

Fish:

8 (4-ounce) fillets fresh cod, skinned, held at room temperature

5 sprigs thyme

Sauce:

3 tablespoons extra virgin olive oil

2 cups sliced Spanish onions

2 cloves garlic, peeled and sliced

1 small zucchini, cut into half-moon slices

3 fresh, ripe tomatoes, stemmed and diced

1 cup sliced olives

2 tablespoons capers, drained

2 tablespoons thyme leaves, freshly chopped

2 tablespoons fresh flat leaf Italian parsley, coarsely chopped

Salt and white pepper

2 cups arugula, rinsed and drained

TO MAKE THE POACHING LIQUID: Place a 3-quart saucepan on the stovetop over high heat and add 6 cups of water, the wine, tea bags, orange, garlic, and thyme. Season with salt and pepper. Bring everything to a boil, then lower the temperature on the stovetop to low heat and simmer for 10 minutes.

TO POACH THE FISH: Place the fillets side by side in a heatproof, 2-inch deep dish. Season with salt and pepper. Lay the thyme in the dish alongside the fillets.

Strain the hot liquid directly over the cod fillets, making sure they are completely covered. Let the cod "cook" in the hot liquid for about 15 minutes, until the flesh is firm. At this point the fish should be perfectly poached. That's it, really! If you are not serving right away, cover the dish and refrigerate the fish in the poaching liquid for up to two days.

TO MAKE THE SAUCE: Place an 8-inch sauté pan on the stovetop over medium heat and add the oil. Once the oil is hot, add the onions and cook until they take on some good color, about six minutes.

Add the garlic and then cook for another two minutes.

Add the zucchini, tomatoes, olives, and capers and cook for about five minutes, until the vegetables soften and release some of their juices. Add the herbs and season with salt and pepper.

If you are not using the sauce immediately, it can be held in the refrigerator for up to two days and then reheated or served cold.

When ready to serve, place a small amount of arugula on each plate, top with a piece of the cod and then spoon the sauce over the fish. A drizzle of extra virgin olive oil over the entire plate will finish this off nicely.

Serve the halibut with poached lemon slices and sprinkled with the remaining parsley. An additional sprinkle of salt at the end will do the dish justice as well.

Olive Oil–Poached Halibut

Eeewww!! Fish poached in oil!!!! Feel better now that you've gotten that out of your system? Not only does this method produce an incredible and not greasy result, it is an easy and healthy way to poach halibut, salmon, or any other thick-fleshed fish.

6 (6-ounce) 1-inch-thick pieces fresh halibut

Salt and white pepper

3 lemons, washed, dried and cut crosswise into thin slices

½ cup capers, rinsed and coarsely chopped

1 cup fresh flat leaf (Italian) parsley, leaves only, coarsely chopped, divided

4 cups extra virgin olive oil

Preheat the oven to 240°F. Position a rack in the center of the oven.

Lay the fish on a paper towel-covered plate. Pat the fish dry on both sides and season with the salt and white pepper.

Layer the lemon slices along the bottom of a glass 9 by 13-inch baking dish. Place the fish fillets on top of the lemons making sure to leave space in between the fillets. Sprinkle with the capers and half of the parsley, and then cover the fish with the oil. Wrap the baking dish tightly with aluminum foil and bake in the oven for 45 minutes to one hour. When done, the fish should be an opaque white and flake easily. When ready, remove the fish from the oven and discard the poaching liquid.

PAN-FRIED FLOUNDER

SERVES 6

Simple, classic, perfect. I have always said that I could fry anything and make it taste good. Well, take some fresh local flounder or fluke and follow this recipe, you may actually be able to convert the whiny ones in the house who insist that they just don't like fish. I pair it with Israeli couscous at the restaurant. A hollandaise or any mayonnaise-based sauce will also make for the perfect accompaniment.

6 (6-ounce) fillets fresh flounder or fluke
Salt and white pepper
2 cups instant or all-purpose flour

6 large eggs, beaten
½ cup extra virgin
olive oil, divided

Line a baking sheet with paper towel. Lay the flounder fillets side by side on the baking sheet and pat dry. Season both sides of the fish with salt and pepper.

Place the flour in a large bowl and season with salt and pepper, because as Emeril Lagasse would say, "I don't know where you buy your flour, but where I buy mine, it don't come seasoned." Isn't he just adorable?

Place the eggs in a large bowl and season them as well.

Place a 10-inch, straight-sided skillet on the stovetop over medium heat and add the oil.

While the pan is heating, coat the fish. First, dredge one fillet in the flour, removing and knocking off any excess. Next, dip the fillet into the beaten eggs, making sure the fillet is fully coated before allowing the excess egg to drip off. Then, completely dredge the fillet in the flour a second time, patting off any loose flour. Set aside on the baking sheet while you repeat with the remaining fillets.

When the skillet is hot, add the fillets one at a time and brown the bottoms. You may need to do this in batches to avoid overcrowding the pan. Use a fish spatula (don't have one, you should get one) to gently flip the fish over to brown the other side. The fish should be cooked perfectly once you get proper color on both sides.

Drain the cooked fillets on a paper towel-covered plate to remove any excess oil. Season one more time with the salt and pepper, and serve hot.

Black Sea Bass in Fine Herb Broth with Green Bamboo Rice

Serves 6

Green bamboo rice is not a new, oddly colored rice. It is a short grain rice that has been infused with the juice of a young bamboo plant. When cooked, the rice is a pale green and a perfect complement to light fish dishes. It is also sometimes used as a sushi rice.

2 cups green bamboo rice

4 cups vegetable or fish stock

1 tablespoon fresh chives,
coarsely chopped

1 tablespoon fresh chervil,
coarsely chopped

1 tablespoon fresh tarragon,
coarsely chopped

1 tablespoon fresh flat leaf (Italian)
parsley, coarsely chopped

Salt and white pepper

6 (6-ounce) fillets black sea bass, skin on

TO MAKE THE BAMBOO RICE: Place a 4-quart, lidded saucepan on the stovetop over medium heat, add 3 cups of water and bring to a boil. Stir in the rice and bring everything back up to a boil. Lower the temperature on the stovetop to low heat and bring the mixture to a simmer. Cover and cook for 12 to 15 minutes, until most of the water has been absorbed. Turn off the heat and let the rice sit covered, for an additional five to 10 minutes. Remove the lid and fluff the rice with a fork.

Place a 3-quart saucepan on the stovetop over high heat, add the stock and bring to a boil. Season with salt and pepper, and mix in the herbs.

Place the fillets side by side in a deep, 9 by 13-inch baking dish. Pour the hot stock over the fish to cover completely. Let the fish poach in the hot stock for 10 minutes. Remove the fillets from the broth, discarding the poaching liquid. Serve the fillets over the bamboo rice.

SAUTÉED FILLET OF COD, CARAMELIZED ONION SAUCE, AND SMASHED OLIVE-OIL POTATOES

SERVES 6

I beg of you, when referring to this fish, it's called cod. *Not* codfish. *It just one more thing that makes me insane. And* FYI, *the* l *is silent in* salmon.

Sauce:

8 tablespoons (1 stick / ½ cup) unsalted margarine

3 tablespoons extra virgin olive oil

2 medium-sized Spanish onions, peeled and thinly sliced

4 cloves garlic, peeled and sliced

4 cups fish stock

4 sprigs thyme

¼ cup apple cider vinegar

Salt and white pepper

Potatoes:

2 pounds Red Bliss potatoes

3 tablespoons extra virgin olive oil

Coarse sea salt and freshly ground black pepper

Cod:

3 tablespoons extra virgin olive oil

6 (6-ounce) fillets fresh cod, skin on

Salt and white pepper

TO MAKE THE SAUCE: Place a 3-quart saucepan on the stovetop over medium-high heat, and add the margarine, oil, and onions. Cook, stirring occasionally, until the onions have caramelized very well. This may take anywhere between 15 to 20 minutes. Add the garlic and cook for another four to five minutes. Pour in the fish stock, add the thyme and cook until the liquid has reduced by half.

Once reduced, add the vinegar and then cook for another five minutes. Strain the sauce through a fine mesh sieve. Use a spatula to press down on the solids to extract as much as possible of the liquid and flavor. Discard the solids. Pour the sauce into a 2-quart saucepan placed on the stovetop over medium-high heat and cook until the sauce has reduced to 1 cup. Season with salt and pepper and keep warm until ready to serve.

The sauce can be made up to three days in advance, cooled and stored in the refrigerator. Gently reheat in a saucepan on the stovetop when ready to use.

TO MAKE THE SMASHED POTATOES: Preheat the oven to 450°F. Place the potatoes on a baking sheet and generously coat them with oil, salt and pepper. Place the baking sheet in the oven and roast the potatoes for about 35 minutes, or until they are very tender. Place the potatoes in a large bowl and while still hot, smash them with the back of a fork, then drizzle with oil and season with salt and pepper. Cover loosely with plastic wrap and keep warm until ready to serve.

TO MAKE THE FISH: Preheat the oven to 400°F. Place a nonstick, 3-quart sauté pan on the stovetop over medium-high heat and add the oil. Season the fillets with salt and pepper. Place three fillets in the pan, skin side down, and cook until the skin is very crisp, about five to six minutes. If the skin sticks to the bottom of the pan, the fillet is not ready. Once the skin has been crisped, place the seared fish on a clean baking sheet while you repeat the process with the remaining three fillets. When all of the fish has been seared, place the fillets in the oven and bake for six minutes.

To serve, place a small mound of smashed potatoes in the middle of each plate, top with a cod fillet and drizzle with sauce.

SAUTÉED FILLET OF WILD SALMON WITH FRENCH GREEN LENTILS

SERVES 6

Salmon:

6 (4-ounce) fillets Wild Alaskan Salmon, skin on

4 tablespoons peanut oil or extra virgin olive oil

Salt and white pepper

Lentils:

4 tablespoons extra virgin olive oil

1 medium-sized yellow onion, peeled and cut into ¼-inch dice

1 small carrot, peeled and cut into ¼-inch dice

1 rib celery, cut into ¼-inch dice

½ small fennel, bulb only, cleaned and cut into ¼-inch dice

1 (16-ounce) box French green lentils

Salt and white pepper

3 tablespoons flat leaf (Italian) parsley, freshly chopped

2 tablespoons tarragon leaves, freshly chopped

Whole-grain mustard vinaigrette:

4 tablespoons whole-grain mustard

2 tablespoons red wine vinegar

1 small shallot, peeled and minced

1 tablespoon honey

6 tablespoons extra virgin olive oil

Salt and white pepper

TO MAKE THE FISH: Preheat the oven to 400°F.

Place the fillets, skin side up, on a clean work surface. Use a sharp knife to gently score three diagonal marks into the flesh of each fillet. You want to just slice through the skin without making a deep cut in the flesh. Score the skin from edge to edge to prevent the fillets from curling up in the pan.

Place a nonstick, 8-inch, ovenproof skillet on the stovetop over medium heat and add the oil. Season the fish on both sides with salt and pepper. Add the fish to the hot pan skin side down and cook until the skin crisps up, about four minutes. Place the pan in the oven and bake for another four minutes. You want the center of the fish to be just barely cooked through.

TO MAKE THE LENTILS: Place a large shallow pan, (this can be either a large frying pan or a sauté pan with straight sides) on the stovetop over medium heat and add the oil. When the pan is hot, add the onions, carrots, celery, and fennel and cook until softened. Stir in the lentils and cook for one more minute. Season with salt and pepper, and add enough water to cover the mixture by ½ inch. Lower the temperature on the stovetop to low heat and cook until all of the water is fully absorbed and the lentils are tender, approximately 30 minutes. Fold in the herbs just before serving.

The lentils can be made up to three days in advance, if cooled and stored in the refrigerator. Reheat before serving.

TO MAKE THE VINAIGRETTE: Place the mustard, vinegar, honey, and shallots in a bowl and whisk to combine. Add the oil in a slow stream while whisking vigorously. Season with salt and pepper.

To serve, place some warm lentils in the center of each plate and top with a salmon fillet, skin side up. Drizzle with a small amount of vinaigrette.

SEARED YELLOWFIN TUNA BASQUAISE

SERVES 6

The only part of this that will trip you is before you even hit the kitchen. That's finding a reputable fishmonger, finding fresh tuna (frozen sucks, save your money), and then having them cut the tuna into the way that you want it. If need be, a tuna steak will do. But make the fish dude work for his $25 a pound, don't accept what is already cut and sitting in the case for who knows just how long.

Remove the tuna from refrigerator and allow the fish to come up to room temperature. A good 15 minutes or so should do the trick.

1½ pounds Yukon Gold fingerling potatoes

Salt and white pepper

3 tablespoons extra virgin olive oil

3 red bell peppers, de-ribbed, seeded, and cut into thin slices

1 yellow bell pepper, de-ribbed, seeded, and cut into thin slices

2 medium-sized yellow onions, peeled and thinly sliced

8 cloves garlic, peeled and thinly sliced

8 sprigs thyme

2 cups dry white wine, chardonnay will work well

6 (6-ounce) portions yellowfin tuna, square cut, skinned

Garnish:

Juice of 2 lemons

Extra virgin olive oil

4 sprigs flat leaf (Italian) parsley, leaves only

Place a 3-quart saucepot on the stovetop over medium heat and add the potatoes. Add enough cold water to cover the potatoes and bring to a boil. Lower the temperature on the stovetop to low heat and bring to a simmer. Cook until a knife inserted into the center of the potatoes comes out easily. When fully cooked, drain off the hot water and immediately submerge the cooked potatoes in a bowl of cold water; this will stop the cooking process. When the potatoes are cold to the touch, drain off the water and cut the potatoes into workable sized wedges.

Place an 8-inch sauté pan on the stovetop over medium-high heat and add the oil. Working in batches, add the potato wedges and cook until well browned. Season with salt and pepper and set aside on a paper towel-covered plate.

Once all of the potatoes have been browned, add another 2 tablespoons oil to the pan. When the oil is hot, add the peppers and onions and cook until softened and browned. Add the garlic and cook for additional three minutes. Season the vegetables with salt and pepper. Add the thyme and the wine, lower the temperature on the stovetop to low heat and bring to a simmer. Once all of the vegetables are fully cooked through, lower the temperature on the stovetop and keep the vegetables warm while you sear the tuna.

Place a nonstick, 8-inch sauté pan on the stovetop over high heat and add 1 tablespoon of oil. Season the fish with salt and pepper. When the oil begins to smoke, quickly sear the fish on all sides (see note). You want the tuna to be very rare at this point, as it will be cooked a second time.

[SIDENOTE: The searing is a fast process so be prepared before you start; this is no time for slacking off. The goal is to develop some fast color and flavor, so no more than 30 seconds per side should suffice.]

Add the seared tuna to the sauce simmering on the stovetop, and baste the fillets with the sauce. Let cook at a simmer for no more than three to four minutes, allowing just enough time for the tuna to absorb some flavor, but not enough time to let it overcook. Remove the tuna from the pan and set on a clean cutting board. Use a very sharp knife to cut each fillet into ½-inch-thick slices. If the tuna has been cooked properly, it should be nice and red in the center. If the center is grey, then you overcooked the tuna, and you have brought me great shame.

To serve, spread some vegetables out in the center of each plate and top with the tuna slices. Drizzle with lemon juice and oil, and garnish with a sprinkling of parsley.

WHOLE ROASTED SALT-CRUSTED RED SNAPPER

SERVES 2

Despite what you may think about anything salt crusted, the fish doesn't become as salty as a kosher hanger steak. To the contrary. The result – that is, if you don't overcook it – should be most flavorful and perfectly seasoned.

1 medium-sized lemon

3 pounds kosher salt

3 sprigs thyme, divided

3 sprigs flat leaf (Italian) parsley

4 large egg whites

1 whole red snapper (about 4 pounds), scaled, gutted, fins removed

1 fresh bay leaf

Preheat the oven to 450°F.

Use a vegetable peeler to peel the lemon rind into strips. Cut the lemon into rounds and set aside.

Place the lemon rind, salt, half of the thyme, and all of the parsley in the bowl of a food processor fitted with the blade attachment and process until very well combined. Add the egg whites and process until well incorporated.

Line a baking sheet with parchment paper. Spread about one-quarter of the salt mixture on the baking sheet, so that it covers an area approximately one inch wider and longer than the size of the fish. Place the fish on top of the salt. Open up the fish and line the cavity with the lemon slices, the remaining thyme, and the bay leaf. Pack the rest of the salt mixture on top of the fish, making sure to spread the salt evenly over the top and sides. The surface should be as smooth as possible to ensure even cooking.

Place the baking sheet in the oven and roast the fish for about 20 to 25 minutes, until a thermometer in-serted into the center of the fish reads between 120°F and 125°F. This will yield a flaky, succulent fillet.

[SIDENOTE: To check for doneness, insert either the tip of a paring knife or a metal skewer into the center of the fish and hold it there for five to 10 seconds. Remove the knife and gently place the blade against your bottom lip. If the blade is warm to the touch, the fish is ready. This is an old-school method, but it works. If kickin' it old school doesn't do it for you, use the thermometer.]

Use the back of a chef's knife to crack open the salt crust and pull it away from the fish. Use a fork or fish spatula to lift off the top fillet and place it on a serving platter. Use a fork to gently remove the back-bone from the remaining fillet and discard. Gently place the deboned fillet on the serving platter.

Don't forget the head; put the head on the plate as well. The head and cheek meat is the best flavored on the fish. Save the eyeballs; it is a Portuguese tra-dition to serve them to your most esteemed dinner guest.

Sides

The sides sell the dish. Period. It's true in the restaurant and it's equally as sure at your dinner party or family event. Unfortunately, most believe that they are nothing more than an afterthought to the star of the plate. Let's put it this way, as great as Al Pacino and Marlon Brando were, what would the *Godfather* have been without Sonny, Fredo, and Tom Hagen.

RED CABBAGE SLAW

SERVES 8

This is the perfect acidic complement to fish, steak, or BBQ. It also can and should be made at least three hours in advance, giving the salad a chance to marinate so that the flavors can develop.

1 head red cabbage, rinsed and thinly cut into 2-inch slices

2 medium-sized carrots, peeled and thinly cut into 2-inch slices

1 medium-sized red onion, peeled and thinly cut into 2-inch slices

1 teaspoon caraway seeds

1 bunch cilantro, leaves only

1 bunch scallions, coarsely chopped

½ cup fresh mayonnaise (page 18)

¼ cup Dijon mustard

3 tablespoons honey

3 tablespoons lemon juice

Salt and white pepper

Place the cabbage, carrots, red onion, caraway seeds, cilantro leaves, and scallions in a large bowl and toss to combine.

Place the mayonnaise, mustard, honey, lemon juice, salt and pepper in a small bowl and whisk until incorporated.

Toss the salad with the dressing and refrigerate for three hours before serving. If you want to make this in advance, my recommendation is that you prep all of the vegetables, cover them with plastic wrap and then leave in the refrigerator overnight. Then proceed as directed above.

ROASTED CHERRY TOMATOES, GARLIC, AND PINE NUTS

SERVES 8

I love the simplicity of this side dish. In late August when tomatoes are at their peak, roast them on the vine.

3 bunches cherry tomatoes (about 2 pints), on the vine if available, rinsed

4 cloves garlic, peeled and cut into thin slices

½ cup pine nuts

6 sprigs thyme

2 tablespoons extra virgin olive oil

Salt and freshly ground black pepper

Preheat the oven to 400°F.

Place the tomatoes in a bowl with the garlic, pine nuts, olive oil, thyme, salt and pepper and toss to combine. Spread the tomatoes out onto a clean baking sheet and roast them in the oven until the tomatoes are brown, with some parts even beginning to almost burn.

HARICOT VERT

SERVES 6

Haricot vert are French green beans. They are thinner and a bit more complex tasting than the standard green bean. You can prepare these in advance: do the blanching step only and then reserve them in the refrigerator, for up to two days, until you are ready for the final sauté, or "pick up" as we fancy chef types call it.

Kosher salt

1 pound fresh haricot vert, stemmed

2 tablespoons extra virgin olive oil

2 small shallots, peeled and thinly sliced

Zest of 1 lemon

3 tablespoons freshly chopped flat leaf (Italian) parsley

Salt and white pepper

Place a 3-quart saucepan on the stovetop over high heat and fill about half full with water. Add a generous amount of salt to the water and bring it to a boil. The salt will season the beans and preserve their bright green color. When the water comes to a rolling boil, add the beans and boil until they are tender, but still have a slight snap; think of al dente pasta.

Remove the haricot vert from the hot water and immediately submerge them in a bowl of ice water to stop the cooking. When cooled all the way through, drain the beans and dry on a towel to remove as much water as possible. If the beans absorb too much water they will taste waterlogged.

Place an 8-inch skillet on the stovetop over medium heat and add the oil. Add the shallots and cook until soft and translucent. Stir in the blanched beans and cook for an additional five minutes, until the beans crisp up with very slight browning. If the beans blister slightly, that's OK. Stir in the lemon zest and chopped parsley and season with salt and pepper. Serve immediately.

SALSIFY

SERVES 8

Salsify is a root vegetable belonging to the dandelion family; salsify is also known as the oyster plant because of its oysterish taste when cooked (just trust me on this one). The root is similar in appearance to a long, thin parsnip, with creamy white flesh and a thick skin. Like many root vegetables, salsify can be boiled, mashed, or used in soups and stews. This is how I like it.

2 pounds salsify

2 tablespoons extra virgin olive oil

2 medium-sized shallots, peeled and thinly sliced

Salt and white pepper

2 tablespoons (¼ stick / ⅛ cup) unsalted margarine or butter

4 sprigs thyme

Fill a large bowl with cold water and set aside.

Use a vegetable peeler to peel the black bark from the salsify. Cut the salsify into quarters and hold them in the cold water until ready to cook. This will keep the salsify from oxidizing, or turning brown. The salsify can be peeled and held in the water overnight.

Place an 8-inch skillet on the stovetop over medium heat and add the oil and shallots. Drain the water from the salsify and pat the salsify dry. Add the salsify to the pan and cook for about eight minutes, until fork tender. Season with salt and pepper. Add the margarine and thyme, and baste the salsify with the melted fat for an additional three minutes, or until the salsify turns golden brown. Serve immediately.

Braised Fennel, Apples, and Onions

Serves 8

A surprisingly simple to make and yet still complex side that works well with firm-fleshed fish and veal.

2 tablespoons extra virgin olive oil

2 medium-sized fennel, bulbs only, cleaned and cut into 1-inch slices

1 medium-sized Spanish onion, peeled and cut into 1-inch slices

2 cups white wine, such as chardonnay

2 cups water

1 small bunch thyme

1 large Granny Smith apple, peeled, cored and cut into 1-inch slices

Salt and white pepper

Place a 10-inch, straight-sided skillet on the stovetop over medium heat and add the olive oil. Add the fennel and onions and cook until browned and caramelized, about eight minutes. Season with salt and pepper. Add the wine, water, and thyme. Lower the temperature on the stovetop to low heat and simmer for about 15 minutes, until the fennel starts to become tender.

Stir in the apples and simmer for another seven minutes. You want the fennel to be tender and the apples cooked through yet firm. Season as necessary and serve.

If making in advance, cool the vegetables in their liquid. They can be held for up to three days and then reheated.

RATATOUILLE

SERVES 8

This is a vegetable stew from the south of France, Provence to be exact. It should be made in the summer when the squash are at their best and are the least bitter and acidic.

1 (28-ounce) can whole plum tomatoes, cut into ½-inch dice, juice reserved

3 tablespoons extra virgin olive oil, plus extra for cooking

2 large red onions, peeled and cut into ½-inch dice

2 heads garlic, peeled and sliced

1 large Italian eggplant, stemmed and cut into ½-inch dice

1 large zucchini, cut into ½-inch dice

1 large yellow squash, cut into ½-inch dice

1 fresh bay leaf

1 small bunch thyme

Salt and freshly ground black pepper

2 tablespoons red wine vinegar

Preheat the oven to 350°F.

Place the tomatoes, their juice, and a sprinkle of olive oil into an ovenproof 9 by 13-inch roasting pan and roast in the oven until the juices have thickened, about 15 minutes. Remove from the oven and set aside until ready to use.

Place a 10-inch, lidded sauté pan on the stovetop over medium-high heat and add the oil. Add the onions and garlic and cook until softened and browned. Add the eggplant and cook for an additional eight minutes. Stir in the zucchini, squash, roasted tomatoes, bay leaf, and thyme, and season with salt and pepper. Cover the pot with its lid and lower the temperature on the stovetop to low heat. Allow the mixture to simmer for 30 minutes, until all the vegetables are cooked through yet still hold their shape.

Just before serving, stir in the red wine vinegar.

You can make the ratatouille in advance, chill it and store it, covered, in the refrigerator for up to four days. It can be reheated in either a hot sauté pan on the stovetop or on a baking sheet in the oven.

POMMES BOULANGÈRE

SERVES 8

*P*repare the entire dish in advance and then pop it into the oven an hour before serving.

¼ cup extra virgin olive oil

8 tablespoons (1 stick / ½ cup) unsalted margarine, plus extra for greasing the pan

4 medium-sized Spanish onions, peeled and thinly sliced

8 large Russet potatoes, peeled and thinly sliced crosswise

8 sprigs thyme, leaves only

Salt and white pepper

Preheat the oven to 375°F. Thoroughly grease a 4-quart baking dish with margarine and set aside.

Place an 8-inch skillet on the stovetop over medium-high heat and add the oil and margarine. Add the onions, season with salt and pepper, and cook until soft and golden brown. Drain the fat from the onions and set both aside, separately, until ready to use.

Place a thin layer of sliced potatoes on the bottom of the prepared dish and season with salt and pepper. Cover with some of the sautéed onions and sprinkle with fresh thyme. Repeat layers using remaining ingredients, ending with potatoes.

Pour the reserved cooking fat over the layers and then add just enough water to cover the potatoes. Place the dish into the oven and bake for 30 to 40 minutes, until all of the liquid has been absorbed and the top has browned. Insert a paring knife into the center of the dish, if it slides in and out without resistance, you're good to go. No resistance, I'll be strong and not add another joke about the French.

When fully cooked, remove the dish from the oven and serve.

Pommes de Terre Sarladaise (Potatoes Sautéed in Duck Fat)

Serves 8

We Americans have a terribly warped view of food. Simply put, processed foods and sugar are the killers, not the natural things that are so demonized by the press and the average nudnik on the street. Duck fat should be used as a fat without guilt. It's low in saturated fat and high in unsaturated fat, making it one of the healthiest animal fats that you can eat. It's the cooking fat of choice in the southwest of France where the rate of heart disease is half that of the rest of France, which is more than half of that of the U.S. Now, I'm not big into any of that fancy book learnin', but that sounds like a big difference to me.

¼ cup rendered duck fat (page 36)

2½ pounds fingerling potatoes, scrubbed and halved lengthwise

3 cloves garlic, peeled and sliced

¾ cup freshly chopped flat leaf (Italian) parsley

Coarse sea salt

Freshly ground black pepper

Place an 8-inch skillet on the stovetop over medium heat and add the duck fat. Once the fat has melted, add the potatoes and toss to coat them in the duck fat. Lower the temperature on the stovetop to medium-low heat and cook until the potatoes are golden brown on the outside and cooked all of the way through.

When the potatoes are a few minutes from being done, add the garlic and toss thoroughly with the potatoes. Cook the garlic for about three minutes, until it turns golden brown.

Toss the potatoes with the parsley, salt and pepper. Serve hot.

THYME-ROASTED SUNCHOKES

SERVES 8

The sunchoke, a.k.a. Jerusalem artichoke, is neither from Jerusalem nor an artichoke. It is a tuber, from the sunflower family, that is a native of North America. It looks like a gnarly little potato, and when cooked has a taste similar to an artichoke heart. It's also loaded with dietary fiber, which makes it a great substitute for potatoes. However, because of its high fiber content, when eaten raw, it also has gotten the nickname of the fartichoke. Just give a fair warning to those loved ones standing downwind, or not.

2 pounds sunchokes

4 tablespoons extra virgin olive oil

8 sprigs thyme, leaves only

Salt and freshly ground black pepper

2 cloves garlic, peeled and sliced

Preheat the oven to 400°F.

Sunchokes in general are pretty dirty, so put them in a colander and wash them thoroughly under cold water. Drain the sunchokes, and use a sharp knife to cut them into 1-inch pieces. Place the pieces in a large bowl and toss with the oil until well coated. Toss in the thyme and season well with salt and pepper.

Spread the sunchokes single layer onto a clean baking sheet and roast in the oven for about 20 minutes. Sprinkle the garlic evenly over the sunchokes and roast for an additional 10 minutes. By then, the sunchokes should be caramelized and fork tender. Remove from the oven and serve immediately.

CLASSIC BREAD STUFFING

MAKES ABOUT 10 CUPS

This is what makes the Thanksgiving meal special for me. Despite the decidedly Thanksgiving flavor and feel, this is a great side during the colder months with any roasted meat or braised dish.

A couple of quick tips. Firstly, if you are planning on stuffing the turkey with the stuffing, do so only just before roasting it. Doing it one day in advance will promote bacteria growth as well as gassy bellies.

6 cups old sourdough bread (a one-pound loaf should do the trick), torn into bite-size pieces

8 tablespoons (1 stick/½ cup) unsalted margarine, plus extra to grease the pan

2 medium-sized onions, peeled and cut into ¼-inch dice

4 ribs celery, coarsely chopped

3 tablespoons freshly chopped sage

2 tablespoons freshly chopped thyme leaves

1 tablespoon freshly chopped rosemary

½ cup freshly chopped parsley

3 cups turkey or chicken stock (see page 3)

2 cups apple cider

Preheat the oven to 325°F.

Arrange the bread in a single layer on a clean baking sheet and bake in the oven until golden brown, about 10 to 15 minutes. Transfer the toasted bread to a large bowl.

Preheat the oven to 400°F. Grease an ovenproof, 10 by 15-inch lidded casserole dish with margarine and set aside.

Place a 10-inch skillet on the stovetop over low heat and add the margarine, onions, celery, and all of the herbs. Cook, stirring, until the vegetables are softened and cooked all of the way through yet with no color. Remove the pan from the stovetop and add the mixture to the bowl with the toasted bread.

Place a 3-quart saucepan on the stovetop over high heat. Add the stock and cider and bring to a boil. Remove the pan from the stovetop, pour half of the liquid into the bowl with the bread mixture and stir to combine. You want all of the bread to be softened all of the way through, yet not a soggy mess. Add more of the hot liquid in stages until this is accomplished. The dryer the bread, the more stock needed.

Place the stuffing in the prepared casserole dish and cover the dish either with its lid or with aluminum foil. Place the dish in the oven and bake the stuffing for about 30 minutes. Remove the dish from the oven, uncover, and return the dish to the oven for about another 20 minutes, or until the stuffing is well browned. When ready, remove the stuffing from the oven and serve.

If you are making the stuffing in advance, prep it up to the point of just before putting it into the oven. Store the stuffing, covered, in the refrigerator for up to two days and then bake as directed.

PURÉE DE POMME

SERVES 8

I will give you 2 versions, the parve and the dairy version. The dairy version is an adaptation of a recipe from the all-star French chef Joel Robuchon. It is simply put, the most painfully magnificent potato dish ever. Yes, ever. I hands down prefer the Yukon Gold potato verses the russet potato. The Yukon Golds are waxy and less starchy than the Russet, and thus more flavorful.

Dairy Purée de Pomme:
2 pounds Yukon Gold Potatoes, similarly sized
1 pound (4 sticks / 2 cups) butter, diced and cold
¼ cup whole milk, hot
Salt and white pepper

Place a 4-quart saucepot on the stovetop over high heat. Add the potatoes, cover with cold water, and bring to a boil. Lower the temperature on the stovetop to medium-low heat and let the potatoes simmer until fork tender, about 35 minutes. Drain the water from the potatoes. Peel the potatoes and push them through a food mill into a 4-quart saucepan. Place the saucepan on the stovetop over low heat and gently cook out any remaining water. Stir the potatoes with a rubber spatula to release any steam. Cook for about 10 minutes, being careful to not scorch or burn the potatoes on bottom of the pan.

When all or most of the water seems to have evaporated, begin adding the butter in stages, folding with a spatula after each addition. This seems like a ton of butter, and it is, but no worries, the potatoes will do their job and absorb it all. Once all of the butter has been incorporated, switch to a whisk to incorporate the milk into the potatoes. Whip the potatoes until they become fluffy. Season with salt and pepper and serve immediately.

Best ever potatoes!

Olive Oil Purée de Pomme:
2 pounds Yukon Gold Potatoes, similarly sized
8 cloves garlic, peeled
¼ cup extra virgin olive oil
Salt and white pepper
1 bunch flat leaf (Italian) parsley, freshly chopped

Place a 4-quart saucepot on the stovetop over high heat. Add the potatoes and garlic, cover with cold water, and bring to a boil. Lower the temperature on the stovetop to medium-low heat and let the potatoes simmer until fork tender, about 35 minutes. Drain the water from the potatoes and garlic, reserving 1 cup of the cooking liquid. Peel the potatoes and push them, along with the garlic, through a food mill into a 4-quart saucepan. Place the saucepan on the stovetop over low heat and gently cook out any remaining water. Stir the potatoes with a rubber spatula to release any steam. Cook for about 10 minutes, being careful to not scorch or burn the potatoes on bottom of the pan.

When all or most of the water seems to have evaporated, use a whisk to incorporate the oil. If the potatoes are too thick, whisk in some of the reserved cooking liquid until the potatoes reach your desired consistency. Season with salt and pepper, fold in the chopped parsley and serve.

These can be made one day in advance and then reheated in a dry sauté pan before serving.

CHESTNUT STUFFING

MAKES ABOUT 10 CUPS

Everyone has thoughts as to what constitutes a proper Thanksgiving stuffing. I didn't grow up on this; I have, however, grown to appreciate and really enjoy the chestnut version. What I haven't yet come to appreciate is other people's thoughts. One day, maybe. Probably not.

6 cups day old bread (about 1½ large baguettes), torn into bite-size pieces

8 tablespoons (1 stick / ½ cup) unsalted margarine, plus extra to grease the pan

2 medium-sized Spanish onions, peeled and cut into a ¼-inch dice

4 ribs celery, coarsely chopped

3 tablespoons freshly chopped sage

2 tablespoons freshly chopped thyme leaves

1 tablespoon freshly chopped rosemary

½ cup freshly chopped parsley

¾ pound cooked whole chestnuts (about 2 cups), coarsely chopped

¾ cups chicken stock (page 3)

¼ cup apple cider

Preheat the oven to 325°F.

Arrange the bread in a single layer on a clean baking sheet and bake in the oven until golden brown, about 10 to 15 minutes. Transfer the toasted bread to a large bowl.

Preheat the oven to 400°F. Grease a 2-quart lidded casserole dish with margarine and set aside.

Place a large 10-inch skillet on the stovetop over low heat and add the margarine, onions, celery, and all of the herbs. Cook, stirring, until the vegetables are cooked all of the way through, yet without color. Remove the pan from the heat and add the mixture to the bowl with the toasted bread. Add the chestnuts and mix gently to combine.

Place a 2-quart saucepan on the stovetop over low heat. Add the stock and cider and bring to a boil. Remove the pan from the heat. Pour the stock into the bowl with the bread mixture and stir to combine.

[SIDENOTE: you may need to adjust the amount of liquid based upon the bread type used and your desired consistency. If you like your stuffing on the moist side, kind of like a savory bread pudding, add an additional ½ cup of chicken stock and 2 tablespoons of melted margarine. If you want it drier, remove ¼ cup of the liquid.]

Place the stuffing in the prepared casserole dish and cover the dish either with its lid or with aluminum foil. Place the dish in the oven and bake the stuffing for about 30 minutes. Remove the dish from the oven, uncover, and return the dish to the oven for about another 15 minutes, or until the stuffing is well browned. When ready, remove the stuffing from the oven and serve hot from the oven.

[SIDENOTE: To use fresh chestnuts, you will need the kind of patience that I am not equipped with. But if you insist, here's how to prepare them:

Start with one pound of fresh chestnuts. Use a sharp knife to cut an X on the round side of each chestnut. Spread the chestnuts out single layer on a baking sheet, add ¼ cup of water, and bake the chestnuts in a preheated 450°F oven for 10 minutes, or until the shells open.

When ready, remove the chestnuts from the oven and carefully shell and peel them while they are still hot.]

Desserts

Have your dessert, go ahead. If you don't have room at the end of your meal for a bite of dessert, than rethink the way you ate the rest of the day. It makes you feel happy, so don't deny yourself. A big plus of dessert at a dinner party is that once the dessert hits the table and the smell of coffee permeates the air, that's the unspoken signal for find your coats, it's time to go home.

Desserts gives us that one last opportunity to show off our skills before they head out to the car and have the inevitable conversation of grading your efforts. Make up for overcooking the rib roast by serving the perfect warm chocolate cake, immaculate fruit tarts, or crispy topped crème brule.

Crème Brûlée

MAKES 10 INDIVIDUAL CUSTARDS

A cup, a quart, six to eight yolks. This was banged into my head at the CIA as the basic recipe for vanilla sauce, vanilla ice cream, or basic custard base. Unfortunately, it doesn't translate exactly into nondairy baking. This recipe works remarkably well, so much so that you won't miss the dairy, too much. Get a butane torch either at a baking supply store or do what many chefs do – head over to Home Depot.

3 vanilla beans	18 large egg yolks
1 quart unflavored, nondairy coffee creamer	1 cup granulated sugar
	10 tablespoons light brown sugar
¼ cup whipped topping	10 shallow crème brûlée dishes

Use a sharp paring knife to split the vanilla beans in half lengthwise and scrape out the beans. Place a 4-quart saucepan on the stovetop over low heat and add the vanilla beans and pods, the creamer, and the whipped topping. Add half of the granulated sugar and bring to a simmer. Do not boil or the creamer and the whipped topping will separate. Simmer for about 10 minutes, just long enough to bring out the flavor of the vanilla bean.

Place the egg yolks and the remaining granulated sugar in a large bowl and whisk very well until the egg yolks turn pale yellow and are slightly foamy. Slowly whisk the hot mixture into the eggs, whisking constantly to prevent the hot liquid from cooking the yolk; you don't want to scramble the eggs. When fully combined, remove the vanilla bean pods and discard.

Preheat the oven to 300°F. Place the crème brûlée dishes on a baking sheet with a 1-inch-high edge.

Fill the baking sheet with enough water to come halfway up the outside of the dishes. Divide the custard evenly among the dishes and then cover the entire pan first with plastic wrap and then with aluminum foil.

Bake in the oven for about 45 minutes, or until the custard is set but still jiggles in the center. Remove the dishes from the oven, and let cool, uncovered, to room temperature. If using the next day, once cooled they can be refrigerated, covered in plastic wrap. Remove them from the refrigerator one hour before serving to bring them up to room temperature.

When ready to serve, sprinkle 1 tablespoon of brown sugar over the top of each custard. Carefully run the flame of a kitchen torch over the tops of the custard to caramelize the sugar. Wait a minute until the sugar sets and then serve while still warm.

CANELÉS

MAKES 12 CANELÉS

I first experienced this oddly dark-colored pastry in 1999 when I was on vacation in France and had a number of days on my own in Paris. I spent my days going from shop to shop trying as much as I could without exploding. The key to making canelés properly is patience. Your instincts will tell you to pull this out of the oven before the time I tell you. Leave it in for the whole ride.

A canelé is made traditionally in a fluted copper mold. Let's assume you don't have this. A metal muffin tin will work, as will a 4 oz. disposable soufflé tin.

4 tablespoons (½ stick / ¼ cup) unsalted margarine, melted but not hot, plus extra for greasing the molds

1½ cups unflavored, nondairy coffee creamer

3 cups granulated sugar

1 cup bread flour

2 tablespoons dark rum

1 pinch salt

Preheat the oven to 425°F. Grease the molds very, very well with either margarine or cooking spray.

Place all of the ingredients in the container of an electric blender, cover the blender with its lid and process the mixture until smooth. Pour the batter into the molds, filling each about three-quarters full.

Place the molds on a baking sheet and bake in the oven for at least 45 minutes. You are looking for a rich dark brown color. It's this color and dark cara-melizing that gives the canelé its distinct flavor and character. When ready, remove the molds from the oven and pop each canelé out of its molds as soon as you can. This will allow the exterior to crisp up while keeping the center dense, moist and somewhat custardy.

Once you get the hang of it, you can make chocolate canelés by adding some chocolate chips to the center of each filled mold before baking.

BABA AU RHUM

MAKES ONE 10-INCH CAKE

Cake and booze and fire. Need I say more!

Cake:

2 tablespoons granulated sugar

1 package active dry yeast

4 large eggs

2 cups all-purpose flour

½ teaspoon salt

10 tablespoons (1¼ sticks/5 ounces) unsalted margarine, diced, room temperature, plus extra for baking

⅓ cup black raisins

Glaze:

¾ cup loosely packed dark brown sugar

1½ inches fresh ginger, peeled and cut into ¼-inch rounds

Zest of ½ orange

2 whole cloves

1 cinnamon stick

¾ cup dark rum, divided

TO MAKE THE CAKE: Pour ½ cup of warm (not hot) water into the bowl of an electric mixer fitted with the paddle attachment. Add the sugar and yeast and let it sit, untouched, for at least 10 minutes, until foamy. If it doesn't foam, the yeast is dead and you need to start over.

Turn the mixer to low speed and add the eggs one at a time, mixing until smooth. Slowly add the flour and salt and mix until fully incorporated. Add the margarine a little bit at a time, beating until the batter is smooth. Add the raisins and mix until incorporated. Use a spatula to scrape down the sides of the bowl. Cover the bowl tightly with plastic wrap. Place the bowl in a warm place and let sit until the dough doubles in volume; this should take about one hour.

Grease a 10-cup Bundt pan with softened margarine. Spoon the batter evenly into the pan. Cover the pan

tightly with plastic wrap and allow the dough to double again in size; this should take about one hour.

Preheat the oven to 375°F and position a rack in the middle of the oven.

Remove the plastic wrap from the cake pan and place the Bundt pan in the center of the rack. Bake until the cake is golden brown and firm to the touch, about 35 to 40 minutes. Cool the cake in the pan for 10 minutes, then turn it out onto a wire cooling rack placed over a clean baking sheet and let it cool completely.

TO MAKE THE GLAZE: Place a 3-quart saucepan on the stovetop over medium-high heat and add the brown sugar and 1½ cups of water. Add the ginger, orange zest, cloves, and cinnamon stick and bring the mixture to a boil. Low the temperature on the stovetop to low heat, and cook at a simmer for another eight minutes. Remove the pan from the stovetop and let the glaze cool completely. Strain

the glaze into a clean bowl, discarding the solids. Mix in ½ cup of the rum until combined.

Pour the glaze evenly over the top of the cake, allowing it drip down over the sides and onto the baking sheet. Let the excess drip off for 30 seconds or so, and then carefully pull the baking sheet out from under the rack. Tip the baking sheet and pour the excess glaze into a bowl. Place the baking sheet back under the cake. Re-pour the glaze over the cake to ensure the cake is very well glazed.

TIME FOR THE THEATRICS: Place the glaze-soaked cake on a large serving platter. Pour all of the left-over glaze into an 8-inch sauté pan placed on the stovetop over medium-high heat. Add the remaining ¼ cup of rum to the pan and very carefully tilt the pan to the side to allow the rum to catch on fire. If you aren't using a gas stove, use an 11-inch-long gas lighter to ignite. Cut the cake into slices and serve with spoonfuls of whipped topping.

KUGELHOPF

This Alsatian coffee cake is slightly sweet and briochey. This is the perfect opportunity to pull out that fluted Kugelhopf cake mold that has been sitting in the back of your cabinet. You don't have a fluted Kugelhopf cake mold in the back of your cabinet? Shame on you. Then I suppose that a Bundt pan will have to do. Amateur.

3 cups golden raisins	1 teaspoon baking powder
½ cup brandy	6 large eggs, beaten
4 cups all-purpose flour, plus extra for dusting the pan	1 pound (4 sticks /2 cups) unsalted margarine, room temperature, plus extra for greasing the pan
2 tablespoons freshly ground nutmeg	3 cups chopped pecans
4 ½ cups packed light brown sugar	Confectioner's sugar for dusting

Preheat the oven to 375°F. Grease and flour a 10-inch Bundt pan and set aside.

Place the raisins and the brandy in a microwave-safe bowl, cover with plastic wrap and microwave for 30 seconds on high. Allow the raisins to cool, uncovered, to room temperature.

Place the flour, nutmeg, sugar, and baking powder in the bowl of a stand mixer fitted with the dough hook and mix until combined. With the mixer on low speed, slowly add the eggs. Increase the mixer speed to medium-low and mix until the eggs have been incorporated and the dough is smooth. Slowly add the margarine piece by piece, until all of the margarine has been fully incorporated. Fold in the brandy-soaked raisins and the chopped pecans.

Transfer the dough into the prepared Bundt pan and bake in the oven until the top is golden brown and a skewer inserted into the center of the cake comes out dry, about 20 minutes.

Remove the cake from the oven and unmold the Kugelhopf onto a wire cooling rack. Let the Kugelhopf cool completely. When ready to serve, dust the top of the cake with confectioner's sugar.

PROFITEROLES

The pâté a choux dough can be used to make the profiteroles, filled for cream puffs, or piped out into a cylinder shape for an éclair.

Pâté a choux:

1 cup all-purpose flour

¼ teaspoon salt

8 tablespoons (1 stick / ½ cup) unsalted margarine

5 large eggs

Chocolate sauce:

7½ ounces bittersweet chocolate, chopped

1 cup whipped topping

Filling:

Store-bought vanilla ice cream

Preheat the oven to 400°F. Prepare a pastry bag with a ½-inch plain, round tip. If you don't have a tip, use the pastry bag without the tip. Line a baking sheet with a piece of parchment paper.

TO MAKE THE PÂTÉ A CHOUX: Place the flour and salt in a small bowl and whisk to combine. Place the margarine and 1 cup of water in a 4-quart saucepan over medium-high heat and bring to a boil. Lower the temperature on the stovetop to low heat, add the flour to the pan and use a wooden spoon to vigorously beat the mixture back and forth for about 30 seconds, or until smooth. The dough should begin to pull away from the sides of the pan and form a ball. Remove the pan from the stovetop and let the dough cool for two minutes. One at a time, beat in the eggs until incorporated and the dough is smooth and glossy.

Place the dough in the pastry bag. Pipe 1½-inch mounds onto the prepared baking sheet, allowing for room to spread. Place the baking sheet in the oven and bake for about 12 minutes, until the choux

are golden brown. Once removed from the oven, the choux can be cooled right on the baking sheet.

[SIDENOTE: If you don't have a pastry bag, you could spoon the dough into your desired shapes.]

[SIDENOTE: Once the dough is piped into the desired shape, it can be frozen and stored in the freezer for up to six weeks before baking.]

TO MAKE THE CHOCOLATE SAUCE: Place the chocolate in a large mixing bowl. Place a 4-quart saucepan over medium-high heat, add the whipped topping bring to a simmer. Pour the hot liquid over the chopped chocolate and then whisk until smooth and homogeneous. Use the sauce while warm. If the sauce cools, pop it in the microwave for 15 seconds just to warm it through.

TO ASSEMBLE THE PROFITEROLES: Cut each cooled choux puff in half horizontally. Place a small scoop of ice cream in the bottom half of each puff and cover with the top. Liberally drizzle the profiteroles with the warm chocolate sauce.

Port-Poached Pears

Serves 6

This dessert is just like yours truly. Classic, simple, elegant, and cooingly sexy. If you can't find a quality port, use a less tannic dry red wine and increase the sugar by about ½ cup.

Poached pears:

6 cups Port wine

¾ cup granulated sugar

1 cinnamon stick

2 whole cloves

1 strip orange rind

Juice of 1 orange

8 firm, almost ripe pears, Anjou or Bartlett

Place an 8-quart, lidded stockpot on the stovetop over high heat, add all of the ingredients except the pears, and bring to a boil. In the meantime, peel the pears leaving the stem intact and some of the skin on at the top to give them a more rustic look.

When the liquid comes to a boil, lower the temperature on the stovetop to low heat, bring the liquid to a simmer and add the pears. Cover and let cook for 15 to 20 minutes, until the pears are cooked through yet still firm. Turn the pears in the liquid every five minutes or so to ensure even color and cooking. Remove the pears from the pan and set aside while you finish the sauce.

Increase the temperature on the stovetop to high heat and cook the remaining poaching liquid until it has reduced by about three-quarters, or until it becomes syrupy.

Serve the pears while still warm, topped with premium vanilla ice cream. Drizzle both the pears and the ice cream with the warm sauce.

FRIED APPLE PIES

In the spirit of our sixteenth president, I cannot tell a lie. I do, on occasion, enjoy the artery-clogging experience of gorging on fast food with the kids. My favorite part is the lava-hot filled apple pie at the end. (Don't judge me, you're not so perfect!) Serve with a big scoop of vanilla ice cream.

Dough:

3 cups all-purpose flour

4 teaspoons granulated sugar

1 teaspoon ground cinnamon

1 tablespoon baking powder

½ cup vegetable shortening

¾ cup water

1 large egg

Apple filling:

½ cup loosely packed light brown sugar

1⅓ cups apple cider

1 cinnamon stick

Pinch of kosher salt

Juice of 1 lemon

2 teaspoons powdered gelatin, bloomed (see page 250)

4 Granny Smith or Gala apples, peeled, cored and coarsely chopped

2 teaspoons corn starch

1½ quarts peanut oil, for frying

½ cup granulated sugar

1 teaspoon ground cinnamon

TO MAKE THE DOUGH: Place the flour, sugar, cinnamon, and baking powder in the bowl of a stand mixer fitted with the paddle attachment and mix to combine. Add the shortening in small amounts and mix on low speed until all of the dry ingredients are fully incorporated and form a paste.

Place the egg in a small bowl, add ¾ cup of water and whisk to combine. Slowly add the wet mixture to the flour mixture until it forms a dough and pulls away from the side of the bowl.

Wrap the dough in plastic wrap and let it rest in the refrigerator for at least one hour.

TO MAKE THE FILLING: Place a 2-quart saucepan on the stovetop over medium-high heat. Add the sugar, cider, cinnamon, salt, lemon juice, and bloomed gelatin and bring to a boil. Add the apples and simmer until they are slightly soft, yet still have a bite to them. Remove the apples and set aside in a large bowl to cool. Continue to cook the liquid until it has reduced by half. Lower the temperature on the stovetop to low heat.

Place the cornstarch and a small amount of the hot cider mixture in a small bowl and whisk together to form a smooth paste. Whisk the paste into the hot liquid until combined and the cider mixture begins to thicken, about three minutes. Pour the hot mixture over the apples and allow them to cool, uncovered, in the refrigerator for at least one hour.

TO ASSEMBLE AND COOK THE TARTS: Remove the dough from the refrigerator and place on a clean, lightly floured work surface. Divide the dough into four even pieces. Working with one piece at a time, roll out the dough to ⅛-inch thick. Use a 4-inch ring mold to cut circles from the dough. Place about 1 tablespoon of filling (more if you go bigger) in the middle of each circle and then fold the dough over the filling to create a half-moon shape. Use a fork to crimp the edges of the dough together. Repeat until you have used up all of the dough and filling. Place your pies on a plate or baking sheet, covered with plastic wrap, in the refrigerator to cool and set. The pies can be assembled one day in advance.

Place the sugar and cinnamon in a medium-sized bowl and toss to combine.

Place a 4-quart saucepot on the stovetop over medium-high and add the oil. Insert a candy thermometer and heat the oil until it reaches 350°F. Once at 350°F, reduce the temperature on the stovetop to low heat. Carefully add the pies to the hot oil and fry until golden brown on each side. You may need to do this in batches to avoid overcrowding the pot. Drain the pies on paper towel and toss in cinnamon sugar while still warm.

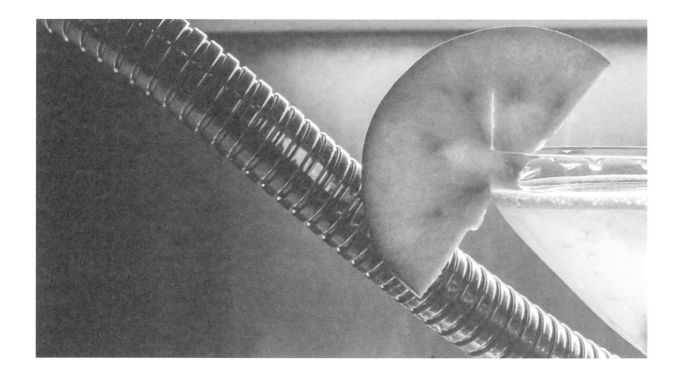

Juliana's Burnt S'mores Tart

Serves 6

The mere thought of s'mores conjures up a warm and fuzzy family campfire scene straight out of a Norman Rockwell painting. I don't know how you grew up, but I never saw a Rockwell painting that showed the kids getting whacked on the back of the head and then told that if you don't shut up, we're turning the car around! Make this for the family, and for just that one moment, that could be you and your family on the cover of the Saturday Evening Post.

Marshmallows:

Peanut or canola oil, for greasing the pan

4 tablespoons powered gelatin

3 cups granulated sugar

1¼ cups light corn syrup

¼ teaspoon salt

2 teaspoons pure vanilla extract

1½ cups confectioner's sugar

Graham-cracker crust:

18 graham crackers

½ cup loosely packed light brown sugar

12 tablespoons (1½ sticks / ¾ cup) unsalted margarine, cut into a ¼-inch dice and frozen

Chocolate ganache:

12 ounces bittersweet chocolate, chopped

1½ teaspoons pure vanilla extract

1¼ cups whipped topping

TO MAKE THE MARSHMALLOWS: Brush a 9 by 13-inch glass baking dish with oil, or spray with cooking spray. Next, line the bottom of the pan with a sheet of parchment paper and brush the parchment paper with oil.

Place ¾ cups of cold water in the bowl of a stand mixer fitted with the whisk attachment and add the gelatin. Allow the gelatin to sit and soften, untouched, while you work on the next step.

Place a 3-quart saucepan on the stovetop over high heat and add the sugar, corn syrup, salt, and ¾ cup of water. Bring the mixture to a boil and insert a candy thermometer. Continue to boil until the sugar mixture reaches 238°F, the softball stage.

When the sugar reaches 238°F, turn on the mixer to low speed and slowly and very carefully pour the hot sugar syrup into the softened gelatin. Once all of the syrup has been added, slowly increase the mixer speed to high. Continue whisking until the mixture becomes stiff; this may take anywhere between 10 to 12 minutes. Add the vanilla extract and whisk until combined. Pour the mixture into the prepared dish and spread it out evenly with an offset spatula. Set aside at room temperature, uncovered, until firm, or for at least two hours.

Sift ½ cup of the confectioner's sugar through a fine mesh sieve onto a clean work surface. Unmold the marshmallow from the baking dish and place onto the prepared work surface. Use a large, sharp knife that has been brushed with oil to cut the marshmallows into 2-inch squares, or into whatever size you prefer. Sift the remaining confectioner's sugar into a bowl and then individually roll each marshmal-

low into the sugar to coat. The marshmallows can be stored in an airtight container for at least one week.

TO MAKE THE GRAHAM-CRACKER CRUST: Place the graham crackers and sugar in the bowl of a food processor fitted with the blade attachment and process until the crackers are finely ground into a powder. Add the margarine and pulse until the margarine is completely incorporated.

TO MAKE THE CHOCOLATE GANACHE: Place the chocolate and the vanilla in a large mixing bowl and set aside. Place a 3-quart saucepan on the stovetop over low to medium heat, add the whipped topping and bring it to a simmer. Pour the hot topping onto the chocolate and whisk until the mixture is smooth and silky. Set aside until ready to use.

TO ASSEMBLE THE TART: Use either one 10-inch tart pan or three to four individual 3-inch tart molds. Pat the graham cracker crust into the bottom and up the sides of the tart pan. Don't be cheap, use all of the graham cracker mix. Next, pour the ganache into the tart shell to fill completely, and use an offset spatula to smooth the top. Place the tart in the refrigerator to set for at least three hours.

TO FINISH THE TART: Completely cover the top of the tart with marshmallows. Just before serving, use a kitchen torch to carefully scorch the marshmallows as much as possible. Be careful not to melt the chocolate; you want the contrast of the cold ganache with the sensation of the warm, scorched marshmallow.

CARAMELIZED QUINCE CHARLOTTE

SERVES 8

Quince is only edible once it has been cooked. So, if you feel like messing with someone you love, tell them that this is just an odd-looking apple and have them take a bite. Be sure, of course, to have the video rolling.

16 tablespoons (2 sticks /1 cup) unsalted margarine, plus extra for greasing the mold

4 pounds quince (about 6 to 8 pieces), peeled, cored and cut into 1-inch cubes or thick slices

2 tablespoons freshly squeezed lemon juice

1 vanilla bean, split

¾ cup granulated sugar

3 tablespoons brandy

1 large brioche or challah loaves (about 12 slices), crusts removed, cut into ½-inch thick slices.

Place an 8-inch skillet on the stovetop over low heat. Add half of the margarine, the quince, lemon juice, vanilla, sugar, and brandy and bring to a simmer. Cook until the liquid has reduced almost all of the way down and the quince are caramelized and tender. Remove from the heat, discard the vanilla bean, and cool completely.

Thoroughly grease a 6-inch Charlotte mold with margarine.

Place a 1-quart saucepan on the stovetop over low heat. Add the remaining 8 tablespoons of margarine and heat until melted. Lay 8 slices of bread on a clean work surface. Use a pastry brush to coat both sides of each slice with the melted margarine.

Cover the bottom of the mold with bread. You may need to use several slices, cutting them to fit and overlapping them slightly. Next line the inside of the mold with the bread, slightly overlapping the slices to look like roofing shingles. Once the mold is fully lined, fill it with the quince filling. Brush the remaining slices of bread with melted margarine and use these to cover the filling. Chill in the refrigerator for 20 to 30 minutes.

Preheat the oven to 400°F. Remove the mold from the refrigerator and bake it in the oven for 30 to 40 minutes, or until the brioche on the top is golden brown. Remember that everything is already cooked. You are baking just for color essentially, so use good judgment.

When ready, remove the Charlotte from the oven and allow it to cool completely before cutting and serving.

Serve with either vanilla ice cream or whipped topping.

LEMON-CURD TART

SERVES 8

Any dessert with lemon makes me happy. The fresh acidity from lemons seems to settle my saturated fat–laden lower intestines and makes for a better night's sleep not only for me, but for my poor wife who has to share the room with me.

Tart shell:

2 cups pine nuts

⅓ cup granulated sugar

3 cups all-purpose flour

1 large egg

1 teaspoon pure vanilla extract

16 tablespoons (2 sticks / 1 cup) unsalted margarine, room temperature

Lemon curd:

3 large eggs

3 large egg yolks

1 cup granulated sugar

¾ cup freshly squeezed lemon juice

9 tablespoons unsalted margarine, cut into ¼-inch dice

Preheat the oven to 350°F.

To make the tart shell: Place the pine nuts and sugar in the bowl of a food processor fitted with the blade attachment and process until finely ground. Add the flour, egg, and vanilla and process until all of the ingredients are fully incorporated. Turn off the machine and use a spatula to scrape down the sides of the bowl as needed. With the processor running, add the margarine several pieces at a time, and process to form a pebbly-textured dough.

Use your fingers to press the dough evenly into the bottom and up the inside of a fluted tart pan with a removable bottom. The dough should not be more than ¼ inch thick. Bake the shell in the oven for 16 to 18 minutes, or until golden brown. Remove the tart shell from the oven and allow to cool at room temperature.

TO MAKE THE LEMON CURD: Place a 6-quart sauce-pan on the stovetop over high heat and fill it about one-quarter full with water. Bring the water to a simmer.

Place the whole eggs, egg yolks, sugar, and lemon juice in a glass or non-reactive bowl and whisk together until very well combined. Place the bowl over the simmering water and cook, whisking continuously, for about eight to 10 minutes, until the mixture has thickened and is a light, lemony yellow color. It should be thick enough to coat the back of a spoon.

[SIDENOTE: When using a double boiler method to gently cook a mixture, remember that the saucepan used to simmer the water should be large enough for the bowl to sit in without allowing the bottom of the bowl to touch the simmering water.]

Add the margarine to the hot mixture piece by piece, fully incorporating between each addition. Once all

of the margarine has been added, remove the bowl from the simmering water. Use a rubber spatula to push and strain the curd through a fine mesh sieve and into a clean bowl. Pour the curd into the cooled tart shell and refrigerate until the lemon curd has set, or for at least two hours before serving.

CARAMELIZED APPLE TART WITH ALMOND CREAM AND THYME

SERVES 8

A fruit tart is the quintessential French dessert, and undoubtedly one of my favorites. Your choice of fruit will depend upon the season. You want to pick the fruit that are at their peak of flavor. In the summer stone fruit will work, in the autumn apples and pears, and in the winter citrus curds work best.

Almond cream:

½ cup sliced almonds

8 tablespoons (1 stick / ½ cup) unsalted margarine, softened

⅓ cup granulated sugar

¼ cup all-purpose flour

1 large egg

Caramelized apples:

3 Granny Smith or Rome Apples, peeled, cored and cut in ¼-inch-thick slices

Juice of ½ lemon

4 tablespoons (½ stick / ¼ cup) unsalted margarine

¼ cup granulated sugar

Tart:

1 sheet puff pastry, frozen

1 small bunch thyme

1 large egg, beaten

TO MAKE THE ALMOND CREAM: Place the almonds in the bowl of a food processor fitted with the blade attachment and process until finely ground. Add the margarine, sugar, flour, and egg and process until smooth. Set aside.

TO MAKE THE CARAMELIZED APPLES: Place the apple slices in a bowl, toss with the lemon juice and set aside until ready to use.

Place a nonstick, 10-inch skillet on the stovetop over medium heat and add the margarine. When the margarine has melted, stir in the sugar and cook, stirring, until the sugar has completely dissolved and begins to turn amber in color. Stir in the ap-

ples and cook, basting often in the rendered liquid, turning the apples once or twice, until the flesh is golden brown and caramelized. Use a slotted spoon to remove the apples and set aside on a plate. Let the apples cool until the tart is ready to assemble. The apples should be caramelized no more than an hour or two before you are ready to use them.

Preheat the oven to 375°F. Place the puff pastry onto a parchment paper-covered baking sheet. Use a fork to poke holes down the center of the dough, where the apples will be placed; this will help release steam as the tart cooks as well as keep the dough from rising too high during baking. Use a spoon or spatula to spread the almond cream over the puff pastry, leaving a 1-inch-wide border around the outside. Layer the sliced apples over the almond cream and top with the thyme. Brush the beaten egg along the border of the puff pastry.

Bake the tart in the oven for about 20 minutes or until all of the puff pastry is brown and crispy. Remove from the oven and allow the tart to cool on a separate plate. It is best served while still warm, yet, still very good at room temperature.

Pistachio and Olive-Oil Cake with Citrus Sabayon and Candied Pistachios

Makes one 8-inch round cake

Cake:

¾ cup extra virgin olive oil, plus extra for greasing the pan

1 cup all-purpose flour, plus extra for dusting

½ cup pistachio flour

2 teaspoons baking powder

1 teaspoon salt

1 cup granulated sugar

3 large eggs

2 teaspoons orange zest

2 teaspoons lemon zest

¼ cup unflavored, nondairy coffee creamer

Candied pistachios:

3 teaspoons granulated sugar

3 teaspoons hot water

½ cup shelled pistachios

2 tablespoons turbinado sugar

Sabayon:

6 large eggs yolks

1 cup citrus-flavored liquor, such as triple sec

⅓ cup granulated sugar

Zest of ½ lemon

Zest of ½ orange

TO MAKE THE CAKE: Preheat the oven to 350°F. Grease an 8-inch diameter cake pan with oil and then lightly dust with flour, knocking out any excess.

Place the all-purpose flour, pistachio flour, baking powder, salt, and sugar in a bowl and mix to combine.

Place the eggs, orange zest, lemon zest, and creamer in the bowl of a stand mixer fitted with the paddle attachment and mix until the batter is light yellow. With the mixer on low speed, mix in the oil until fully incorporated.

Keeping the mixer on low speed, slowly incorporate the dry ingredients.

Transfer the batter to the prepared pan and bake in the oven until a cake tester inserted into the center of the cake comes out clean, about 35 minutes. Allow the cake to cool in the pan for 10 minutes, then remove the cake from the pan and cool completely on a wire cooling rack.

TO MAKE THE CANDIED PISTACHIOS: Preheat the oven to 350°F. Spray a baking sheet with cooking spray.

Place all of the ingredients in a bowl and mix well to combine.

Spread the mixture out onto the prepared baking sheet and bake in the oven for about eight minutes, or until the nuts turn a caramel color.

Let the nuts cool completely and then break them apart by hand. These can be made two days in advance and kept in an airtight container at room temperature.

TO MAKE THE SABAYON: Place an 8-quart saucepan on the stovetop over low heat. Fill the pan one-quarter full with water and bring to a simmer.

Place the yolks, liquor, and sugar in a glass, stainless steel or non-reactive bowl and whisk well to combine.

Make a water bath by placing the bowl over the simmering water (see page 10). Whisking consistently, cook until the mixture becomes rich, thick and foamy. The sabayon is ready when you can run your finger down the middle of the batter and a streak is left behind.

[SIDENOTE: When cooking the sabayon, periodically remove the bowl from the water bath to keep the egg mixture from becoming too hot and cooking the eggs, which will create lumps. The sauce should be hot, but not so hot that you can't comfortably put your finger (clean I hope) into it.]

If you are not using the sabayon immediately, hold it in a thermos until ready to use.

To serve, spoon a small amount of the sabayon onto a plate. Cut a slice of cake and place it over the sauce. Spoon a small amount of sauce over the top of the cake and then sprinkle with candied pistachio.

WARM CHOCOLATE CAKE

MAKES 8 INDIVIDUAL CAKES

I hesitated about putting this into the book. Versions of this have been done so much over the years, I'm almost embarrassed to sell it. It was created in the mid-nineties by the legendary chef Jean-Georges Vongerichten. For him it was a happy accident that was then copied by every nudnik chef on the planet. It was the cronut for 1995.

3 sticks (1½ cups / 12 ounces) unsalted margarine, room temperature, plus extra for greasing the tins

¼ cup all-purpose flour, plus extra for dusting

1 cup granulated sugar

4 large eggs

4 large egg yolks

¼ teaspoon salt

½ pound bittersweet Belgian chocolate, melted and held at body temperature 98°F to 100°F

Confectioner's sugar for dusting

Preheat the oven to 400°F. Grease eight disposable aluminum muffin tins with either margarine or cooking spray and then dust each liberally with flour. Tap out the excess flour and set aside until ready to use.

Place the margarine and the sugar in the bowl of an electric mixer fitted with the paddle attachment and cream together until fluffy. With the mixer on medium speed, add the eggs and the yolks one at a time, incorporating fully after each addition. Add the salt and flour and mix until well combined. Beat in the chocolate until it is just mixed together. Divide the batter evenly among all of the prepared tins.

Place the muffin tins on a baking sheet and bake in the oven for about eight to 10 minutes. The cakes should be baked until the tops of the cakes have just set. Remove the tins from the oven and allow the cakes to rest for three minutes before serving.

When ready, unmold each cake in the center of a plate, dust with confectioner's sugar and serve with either vanilla ice cream or whipped topping.

Opera Cake

Makes one 9 by13-inch cake

Making an opera cake is, quite frankly, a royal pain. Not necessarily complicated, just somewhat of a nuisance. However, if you've got the two things that I usually don't – time and patience – it makes for a great special-occasion cake. It's best to do what I do: let the pastry chef make it. Having 3 baking pans instead of just the one really picks up the pace of the preparation.

Sponge cake:

1½ cups cake flour, plus extra for dusting

18 large eggs

9 cups almond flour

3 ¾ cups sifted confectioner's sugar

18 egg whites

1½ teaspoons salt

9 tablespoons granulated sugar

12 ounces (3 sticks /1½ cups) unsalted margarine, melted

Espresso syrup:

2¼ cups granulated sugar

2¼ cups hot water

5 teaspoons instant espresso powder

Buttercream:

6 large egg yolks

⅓ cup granulated sugar

½ cup room temperature water

12 ounces (3 sticks /1½ cups) unsalted margarine, diced, room temperature

Chocolate glaze:

14 ounces bittersweet chocolate, chopped

12 tablespoons (1½ sticks / ¾ cup) unsalted margarine

Preheat the oven to 425°F. Spray three 9 by 13-inch baking sheets with cooking spray, then line with parchment paper. Spray the parchment paper with cooking spray and then dust with cake flour, knocking out the excess.

TO MAKE THE SPONGE CAKE: Place the whole eggs in the bowl of a stand mixer fitted with the whisk attachment and beat on high speed until the eggs have tripled in volume, about two to three minutes. Turn the mixer speed down to low and add the almond flour and confectioner's sugar, mixing just until they are thoroughly combined. Repeat with the cake flour. If you only have one bowl for the

stand mixer, pour the batter into a large mixing bowl and set aside, and clean and dry the bowl for its next use.

Place the egg whites, salt, and sugar in the bowl of a stand mixer fitted with the whisk attachment and whisk on high speed to stiff peaks. Use a rubber spatula to fold the egg whites into the batter in four additions. Take your time and be gentle, folding until you no longer see white streaks throughout the batter.

Divide the batter evenly among the prepared pans and spread smooth with a rubber or offset spatula.

Place the pans in the oven and bake the cake until golden brown, about 10 minutes. Cool the cakes in the pans.

[SIDENOTE: Because all ovens cook slightly differently, keep an eye on the cakes so they don't over bake.]

Once cooled, unmold the cakes from the pans and set aside until you are ready to assemble. If you have trouble unmolding the cake, it's OK. Save the best one to use as the top layer and just piece together the bottom and middle layers. Nobody is going to see them anyway.

TO MAKE THE ESPRESSO SYRUP: Place a 4-quart saucepan on the stovetop over high heat, add the sugar and water and bring to a boil. Remove the pan from the stovetop and whisk in the espresso powder. Set the syrup aside until ready to use.

TO MAKE THE BUTTERCREAM: Place the egg yolks in the bowl of a stand mixer fitted with the whisk attachment and whisk for two minutes until they are pale in color. Place a 6-quart saucepan on the stovetop over medium-high heat, add the sugar and water and bring to a boil. With the mixer on low speed, slowly and carefully pour the hot syrup into the egg yolks. Keep whisking the mixture for a few minutes until it has cooled down and thickened. This may take between four to six minutes. With the mixer on medium speed, add the margarine one piece at a time until fully incorporated, and the buttercream is thick and smooth.

TO MAKE THE CHOCOLATE GLAZE: Place the chocolate into a non-reactive bowl. Place a 6-quart saucepan on the stovetop over low heat and fill one-quarter full with water. Bring the water to a simmer and cover with the bowl of chocolate to make a double boiler. Once the chocolate begins to slightly melt, use a small whisk to occasionally mix the chocolate until fully melted. This process will take around six minutes.

Piece by piece, begin to whisk in the margarine. Wait until each piece has been fully incorporated before adding the next. The chocolate should be shiny and smooth. Make the glaze as close to the time you will use it as possible. If necessary, keep the glaze warm and covered until you ready to use.

TO ASSEMBLE THE CAKE: Place the first cake layer onto a cake board or serving platter. Use a pastry brush to soak the top of the cake with half of the espresso syrup. Use a large offset spatula to evenly spread half of the buttercream over the espresso-soaked cake. Top the buttercream with the next cake layer and repeat with the remaining espresso syrup and buttercream. Place the nicest looking cake layer on top, bottom side up so that the top is flat. Pour the chocolate glaze evenly over the top, making sure it only covers the top of the cake and does not drip down the sides. Use an offset spatula to smooth and spread the glaze to the edges of the cake layer. If and when the glaze drips down the side, no worries, you could either leave it as is and serve it with that "artisanal look," or trim the edges if you are too sophisticated for that.

Place the finished cake in the refrigerator until the buttercream has firmed up, a few hours or overnight.

This cake is classically cut and served in rectangular slices.

Index

Notes

Notes

Notes

Notes